MOUNTAIN ADVENTURES

A climber on El Capitan.

INTERNATIONAL LIBRARY

KARL LUKAN

MOUNTAIN ADVENTURES

COLLINS · PUBLISHERS FRANKLIN WATTS, INC.

London · Glasgow New York

First Edition 1972
Second impression 1978

ISBN 0 00 100171 X *(Collins cased edition)*
ISBN 0 00 103367 0 *(Collins paperback edition)*
SBN 531 02110 6 *(Watts cased edition)*
SBN 531 02377 X *(Watts paperback edition)*

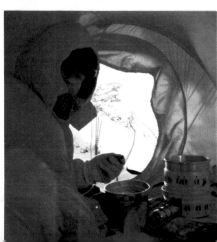

CONTENTS

MAN AND MOUNTAIN

29th May 1953

From a tent pitched at an altitude of over 26,000 feet two men set off to climb Mount Everest, the highest mountain in the world. The thermometer indicates almost 30 degrees of frost. With bearlike ponderousness —after all, their specially designed clothing weighs nearly 17 pounds— they lift their 33 pounds of breathing apparatus on to their shoulders, adjust their face masks, open the valves and take a few deep breaths of oxygen. Then they move off.

One of the men is tall and slender, thirty-three years old. His name is Edmund Hillary (as yet he does not know that on his return from the mountain he is to become *Sir Edmund Hillary*). Hillary is by occupation a bee-keeper.

The other, thirty-nine years of age, was born in the shadow of the highest mountain in the world. He is Sherpa Tenzing and is one of his people's best mountaineers. He has already been a member of six assaults on Mount Everest, the last of which advanced to within 925 feet of the summit.

The path taken by the two men leads over a narrow ridge of ice. To the left and right of the ridge the steep sides fall away down sheer drops of 7,700 feet and 9,300 feet. The two men are like tight-rope walkers high above the abyss.

A sheer cliff face, 30 feet high, can only be surmounted by means of a perpendicular rift between rock and ice. Inch by inch Hillary works his way up it. This, at a height of 27,000 feet! Tenzing follows and— as Hillary puts it later—"collapsed exhausted like a gigantic fish, which, after a fierce struggle, is finally landed".

In spite of their oxygen masks, Hillary and Tenzing have to battle desperately for air to breathe. For breathing apparatus does not provide an inexhaustible source of oxygen and, lacking further containers, Hillary has to cut back on his supply instead of raising it with the increasing altitude.

It was once said by a Himalayan mountaineer that one step forward at this height was equivalent to walking a mile on level ground. Hillary's and Tenzing's advance is not achieved by strolling or walking. Every step must be hacked out of the ice by Hillary with laborious effort and, all the time, the question must arise in his mind, as to how much longer he can endure this struggle.

And then . . . then, at last, Hillary and Tenzing stand at the summit of the highest mountain in the world. They are probably the first men ever to stand there (why only "probably" will be shown later in this book). What are a man's feelings after such a triumphant ascent? Hillary: "My

Dragon in the Rocky Gorge *(Arnold Böcklin, 1870, Schackgalerie Munich). For a long time mountains were regarded as the hideouts of monsters.*

first feeling was one of relief—relief that I did not have to hack out any more steps." 29th May 1953 . . . the world's highest peak climbed for the first time by man!

The number of surmountable peaks in the world, which might attract the sportsman, was once estimated by an historian of the Alps at half a million. No doubt men have already climbed most of them; but there still remains an impressive number of unclimbed peaks. That is an astonishing fact when one considers that the high mountain ranges were visited even by Neanderthal Man.

The Dragon's Lair and its secrets

In 1917 Theophil Nigg, a schoolteacher from Vättis in east Switzerland, and his two sons climbed almost 8,000 feet to reach the Dragon's Lair, where they hoped to find bones of the cave-bear.

The cave-bear was in existence before the onset of the last Ice Age, but did not survive after it. We know that the last Ice Age ended approximately 10,000–11,000 years ago, but nobody could state with any degree of certainty when this began. The period, from 150,000 to 50,000 years ago, had been considered the most likely.

Nigg and his two sons had to dig down to a depth of more than three feet in the hard floor of the Dragon's Lair before they came across the first bones. Beside these they found ashes along with tools of bone and stone. This came as a great surprise. Not only had the cave-bear

Hunting the cave-bear in the Stone Age.

F. ROUBAL 1937

8

The Dragon's Lair near Vättis. A cross-section of the site (from a sketch by the excavators).

made his home in the Dragon's Lair but man had too—Neanderthal Man. For, during the last Ice Age, man could not have survived in the frozen Alps and, after the Ice Age the cave-bear was already extinct. Neanderthal Man must have inhabited Europe at the same time as the cave-bear. It could only have been Neanderthal Man who penetrated so high into the mountains on his hunting expeditions. For him, the meat of a cave-bear weighing 1,120 pounds must have made a great prize. Besides, that rather heavily built animal must have been a relatively easy prey, even with the primitive weapons of those days.

The skull of a cave-bear from the Dragon's Lair, now in the village hall in Vättis.

Even at 4,880 feet in the Wildkirchli Cavern in Switzerland Neanderthal Man once lived. Today there is an inn built into the cavern.

9

During the years between 1917 and 1923 systematic excavations were carried out in the Dragon's Lair. The effort that this represents can only be appreciated by someone who has made the five- to six-hour-long ascent from Vättis to the cave.

Base camp for the excavations was the primitive shepherd's hut on the Gelbberg Alp (6,700 feet). From there, the daily climb to the dank gloom of the excavation site was made. Sometimes the excavators would have to dig two or three yards down into the solid floor of the cave before they reached any fossiliferous layers. Often bad weather forced them to seek refuge in the valley, while on other occasions fresh falls of snow and avalanches rendered the climb to the cave quite impossible. Sundays were spent in Vättis, but on Mondays came the climb back to the site. Two goats were used to supply the excavators with milk and, at the same time, provided the most reliable weather forecast— before every storm they would flee down into the valley.

The efforts of the excavators were richly rewarded. They made a sensational discovery and sparked off a controversy among the experts which, to this day, remains unresolved. They found proof that Neanderthal Man was by no means the primitive being he had so far been considered. What they discovered was a stone vessel, approximately seven feet deep, containing seven well-preserved skulls of the cave-bear. The remnants of the muzzles were all pointing towards the entrance to the cave. It was correctly concluded that these were used as fetishes and that there must have existed, as early as Neanderthal Man, a belief in a higher power, which could even determine the success of hunting trips. This discovery led not only to archaeological

discussions but also to heated theo-
logical debates, and the gloomy
cave, high up in the mountains,
became famed as the oldest shrine
in Europe and probably even in the
world.

Whenever Neanderthal Man
made the ascent to the Dragon's
Lair, he had to have the same sure-
footedness and head for heights,
together with a certain amount of
practice in climbing, that every
visitor today must have. The climb
is given a grade I rating on the
alpine scale of difficulty.

The modern mountaineer recog-
nizes six grades. The sixth is the
most difficult challenge that a mountain can present. But even a grade I
climb requires the skill of a top-
class mountaineer. Many good
mountaineers have plunged to their
deaths while on climbs rated as
only grade I. Thus, Neanderthal
Man was already an accomplished
mountaineer.

A second before midnight

If we were to imagine the history of
the Earth as condensed into the
space of one year, it could be said
that alpine Neanderthal Man did
not appear until a quarter of an
hour before midnight on 31st
December. The Matterhorn and
Mount Everest, too, are very young
in comparison with the age of the
Earth. They are approximately 60
million years old. It is true, however,
that the events which led to the
formation of the first mountain
ranges (such as the emission of flows
of molten rock from within the
Earth, the laying down of sedimen-
tary rock in the primeval sea, and
faults and rifts through movements
of the Earth's crust) extend far back
in time. The first mountain ranges,
formed approximately 500 million
years ago, were levelled long ago by

The 858-foot Devil's
Tower in Wyoming,
U.S.A. Molten rock
from the depths of
the earth solidified to
form this pillar.

An "unnecessary"
message on the top
of the Devil's Tower.

A reminder of the Ice
Age —rocks polished
by glaciers.

A 19th-century impression of an avalanche destroying a mountain village. Only in this century have mountain dwellers learned to safeguard against this danger.

Possible ways of making safe a slope susceptible to avalanches.

erosion, and even today mountains are being worn down.

The epoch in the history of the Earth that is marked by the beginning of the last Ice Age, must have been a period of great hardship for Neanderthal Man, found in the Dragon's Lair. Temperatures dropped lower and lower until eventually he had to resign himself to abandoning his cave-dwelling and seeking refuge in the valleys and the warmer regions below. Slowly but unrelentingly, like huge white dragons, the glaciers crept forward through the valleys. This was the fourth Ice Age to envelop the Earth, and no one today can say for certain that it was the last.

At the start of the warm age in which we now live, the world was populated by a more highly developed species of man. They soon established settlements in the mountains, not only because they represented ideal hunting territory but also because the hillsides provided rich pastures. Later, man learned to exploit the mineral resources to be found there (salt, copper, gold and silver). And today mountains have become marketable as recreation areas for city-dwellers. For thousands of decades the mountain regions have provided an excellent environment for man.

To return to our analogy, the first mountaineers to attempt summit ascents made their appearance only a second before midnight on 31st December. Nevertheless the short history of mountaineering— or "the pursuit of the pointless" as the famous French mountain guide Lionel Terray called it—has been more than compensated for by the intensity of the fascination it has held for people of all nationalities; and today the great adventures of mountaineering have become a part of our heritage.

A mountaineer's tent in the Hindu Kush.

Climbing above the Mediterranean, in the Calaigues at Marseilles, France.

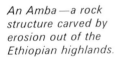

An Amba—a rock structure carved by erosion out of the Ethiopian highlands.

This loess tower, standing by the Dead Sea, is held together by salt. It has been climbed with the help of axes and crampons.

CHAPTER 1

THE THRONES OF
THE GODS

Holy mountains

Anyone who travels in an aircraft knows the experience: cloudy, rainy weather for take-off and then, suddenly, after a few minutes in the air, dazzling sunlight as the plane penetrates a thick blanket of cloud.

A similar kind of experience was shared by men living in mountainous regions many tens of thousands of years ago. Often when climbing on the mountains, a man would suddenly emerge from a grey mist into bright sunlight. Men living farther away from the mountains, on the other hand, would often see only their covering of cloud. The mountains were regarded by one and all as representing something totally different from the valley, and from the very beginning men believed that high mountains must be the homes of superior beings.

According to an Asiatic legend, Paradise itself lies at the top of a mountain. On account of his arrogance, Adam, the first man on Earth, was banished by the gods from the mountains to the valleys below. Many legends tell also of gods who were born high up in the mountains. The Greek god Zeus, the ruler of Heaven, is one example. Jesus Christ, of course, died on Mount Golgotha, and Moses received the Ten Commandments on Mount Sinai. In Japan, Fujiyama is

regarded even today as a holy mountain.

The Mountain of Miracles

Mount Bego in the French Maritime Alps north of Nice, is almost 9,750 feet high. Three or four thousand years ago it was considered by the inhabitants of the Alps to be the home of the gods. A person would climb this mountain to make his special wish known to the gods and, lest the gods forget, each man would draw on the rock beneath the summit symbols which formed a kind of picture language. For example, the head of an ox would mean: May my animals thrive and multiply. The sign of a dagger: May my weapons bring me great victories. The sign of an animal trap: May I find many fine animals caught in my traps.

All of the 40,000 rock drawings so far discovered on Mount Bego have been found at a height of 5,850–8,722 feet. The summit itself is not difficult to reach, but the area in which these drawings have been found stops some distance short of the summit. What could be the reason for this? Was man maintaining a respectful distance between himself and the gods? Or could it be that only the priests were allowed to climb to the summit, as was the case with Moses on Mount Sinai?

Mount Ararat.

On Mount Bego — on this rock the alpine dwellers of the Stone Age carved their requests to the gods.

The story of the discovery of this holy mountain is as extraordinary as the mountain itself. The people who inhabited the area were well aware of the existence of the mysterious rock drawings, and they even referred to the mountain as the Mountain of Miracles. For a long time the drawings were thought to be either hieroglyphics or the scribblings of Hannibal's soldiers, or even secret signs made by devil worshippers. But, at the end of the last century, the Englishman Clarence Bicknell happened to visit this region. He was an amateur botanist and, in his search for rare plants, he actually came across the mysterious pictures drawn on the rocks.

Bicknell gradually forgot his plants and became increasingly interested in these drawings. Eventually the amateur botanist became an historian of distinction. In his book about the rock drawings of Mount Bego, published in 1911, Bicknell wrote: "Day by day the fascination which these rocks held for me grew, as one could expect when one discovers the traces of an unknown people."

Rock carvings on Mount Bego. Symbols for animal traps, heads of cattle and bronze daggers.

A rock carving on Mount Bego. This is the so-called "Magician", a bearded man holding bronze daggers in his outstretched hands.

Mount Ararat and Noah's ark

After the Great Flood, according to the Bible story, Noah and his ark landed on a mountain in Armenia. The Armenians themselves have regarded Mount Ararat as Noah's mountain since Biblical days. They say that the ark still rests at the summit of the mountain and that man is forbidden by the gods to approach the mountain-top.

It is certainly true that excavations in Mesopotamia have proved that there was once a Great Flood, but legends of such floods are a part of the history of different nations in all of the continents. Already 300 different versions of the legend have been identified and they all tell of a man and a woman landing on the top of a mountain in a boat or an ark. At the moment there are supposed to be mountains connected with such a legend in the North American Rockies, in Mexico, in Peru and Chile, in the Fiji Islands, in the Himalayas and so on. But Mount Ararat is still the most famous of all such mountains.

Ararat was first climbed in 1829 by the geographer Friedrich Parrot and seven companions. Parrot was not searching for Noah's ark, but merely wanted to measure the height of the mountain, and that is all he did do. Mount Ararat only started to make headlines in this century, when, flying in the face of all rational thought, various men began to equip serious expeditions to try to find and salvage Noah's ark. Excavations in Mesopotamia had proved the existence of a great flood disaster and why, therefore, should it not be true that Noah's ark really did come to rest on Mount Ararat? Only one thing was overlooked by these men. If, in fact, the volume of flood water had been enough to carry Noah and his ark to a height of 16,500 feet, then only deep borings into the soil of Mesopotamia could really prove the existence of such a catastrophe. Certainly no single excavation could have proved the legend.

Men returned from these expeditions claiming that every piece of wood they had found was an important discovery and the concept "holy mountain" lost much of its value ... until Hias Rebitsch found the silver gods on Cerro Gallan.

Fujiyama (12,395 feet) is Japan's highest mountain and its holy mountain. It is climbed every year by more than 100,000 pilgrims. (Reproduced from a work by Hiroshige.)

Adventure at 19,500 feet

It all began quite harmlessly. Rolf Gallan from Salzburg had told Rebitsch that at the summit of

In the steep rock face on Arbel in Israel are cave strongholds used by the Jews after their rebellion against the Romans in A.D. 66. Some of the caves can only be reached using modern climbing techniques.

Cerro Gallan (about 19,500 feet) he had come across burial monuments. The question was: Who had erected them? Rebitsch would not rest until he had seen these burial monuments for himself, and in 1955 he journeyed to the Andes to do so.

At a height of 15,275 feet his Muli guides began to gasp and choke from lack of oxygen and at 16,200 feet their noses began to bleed. It was left to three men, therefore, to haul the equipment up to a height of 17,220 feet and there to pitch their tent (or the advance camp as it is called in mountaineering terminology). With one companion Rebitsch reached the summit of Cerro Gallan, where he saw the burial monuments. He was fascinated by them and excavations were begun which were to claim a special place in the already rich history of archaeology.

On the very next day Rebitsch left the advance camp alone (for his companion was exhausted) and he climbed once more to a height of 19,500 feet where, equipped only with a spade, he began his archaeological excavation. Rebitsch recounts: "First of all, I threw the heavy rocks from the surrounding wall down the cliff and cleared a passage for the excavated material. Then for a whole day, right through till dusk, I burrowed like a mole, shovelling and digging almost non-stop both with the spade and with my bare hands, until I was drained of all further energy and will power. I consciously taxed my strength to its limits—a dangerous thing to do at this altitude—and I really was on the verge of exhaustion. A cold frenzy had taken hold of me. I ignored my hunger and thirst and was no longer aware of the storm and the cold. Caked in dirt, my face smeared with dust and sweat, and my eyes burning and clogged with grit, I dug and hacked away at the

ground and burrowed deeper. When my arms had reached the end of their endurance I lay on my stomach or my back and pushed the pile of dirt and lava rocks away from me with my legs. It all plunged down the side of the mountain carrying boulders and rubble down with it. The wind whipped up clouds of dust and chased them high up into the sky."

At the top of Cerro Gallan, this lonely archaeologist discovered stone axes belonging to the Incas and silver figurines of their gods—he had uncovered an ancient place of worship! But then something very mysterious happened, as Rebitsch himself relates: "I was still in the tunnel at the summit of Cerro Gallan, but, being so cut off from the outside world, my thoughts

began to wander. I ought to have been at work digging, for the short time I had to complete the job was fast running out. I had scarcely more than half an hour left and still had to explore a few remaining crannies of the tunnel. I had not a minute to lose. It was imperative that I dig on. But for some peculiar reason I began to crawl back towards the entrance—I felt I just had to examine more closely the last statue I had unearthed, now standing outside. It seemed so fascinating. Red shells were a tribute to kings. . . . I backed out of the tunnel ignoring all rational thought, but acting rather as if under the compulsion of some higher power, of some inner command! I stood outside and took the statue in my hand, exasperated now because it seemed so absurd to have succumbed to such emotionalism. I regretted the time wasted by my day-dreaming. I wanted to get back into the tunnel immediately. I knelt down and lowered my head. Then there was a short muffled crack, an explosion and the arched entrance which was before frozen solid disintegrated and the heavy roof of the tunnel collapsed. I stood there stunned. Upon what magic forces had I stumbled, for surely the small statue of the god had intervened to save my life, at the very moment when the fates were deciding whether I should live or die. Had it not been for the statue I would have been lying under the leaden weight of the ruins of the tunnel! It would have been a slow and agonizing death without any prospect of rescue. . . ."

Aconcagua (22,597 feet), the mightiest peak in the Andes — for a long time considered by the natives as the seat of the gods.

CHAPTER 2

THE CONQUERORS
OF THE MOUNTAIN
RANGES

No mountain touches the sky

In 218 B.C. the Carthaginian Hannibal crossed the Alps with an entire army. Having taken one look at the mountains, the soldiers had refused to continue. But according to the Roman historian Livy, Hannibal was able to persuade his men by saying: "The mountains of the Alps indeed reach great heights, but nowhere do they touch the sky and none is impossible to climb. Men live in the Alps and cultivate the land; creatures are born and live there. If individual beings are able to survive there, why not a whole army?"

It was the end of October when Hannibal made his crossing. Already fresh falls of snow covered those of past years and the army made slow progress. Every mountain soldier knows how much quicker progress is for one man alone on a mountain than for a whole group of men, especially if they have elephants with them! Both men and beasts suffered terribly in the icy conditions. The great technical problems involved only diminished once the army began the descent towards the south. As is the case with every alpine crossing, the most difficult terrain was not in the high mountain passes but rather in the deeper areas where water has carved out deep ravines between high mountain walls. Sometimes a path had to be forced through them. . . . "It was necessary to cut through the rock; large trees were felled and a huge pile of timber erected. This was set alight and, when the rock was red-hot, the men's rations of sour wine were poured on it to make it brittle" (Livy). It took four days before even this one short stretch of the way was made passable. In all Hannibal took fifteen days to cross the Alps. When he reached the plains of Italy he thought, according to Livy; "that he had surmounted not only the walls of Italy but also the walls of Rome itself".

Even Livy writes that accounts of the strength of Hannibal's fighting force varied greatly and that some sources mentioned up to 100,000 infantry and 20,000 cavalry. The historian Polybius (200–120 B.C.) records that Hannibal began his journey across the Alps with 38,000 infantry and more than 8,000 cavalry and that he brought only 20,000 infantry and 6,000 cavalry safely across with him. The importance which was attributed to this campaign in ancient times is amply demonstrated by the fact that fifty years after the event Polybius decided to seek out the mountain overcome by Hannibal and his army, purely (as Polybius himself implies) out of his curiosity to see where it all happened.

Alexander the Great, the fearless conqueror of mountains. A section of the famous mosaic from Pompeii, now in the National Museum in Naples.

Hannibal was not the first person, however, to cross a mountain range with a whole army. Almost two centuries before, Xenophon had led a Greek army over the 9,000-foot highlands of Asia Minor in winter. In his book *Anabasis* Xenophon describes this march of the ten

Hannibal crossing the Alps. A pen drawing by Lajos von Horvath.

thousand and the measures that had to be taken to safeguard against snow-blindness and the threat of freezing to death.

Soldiers with wings

Turbulent rivers in uncharted mountain country are as formidable obstacles to modern mountaineers as they were to Alexander.

In the winter of the year 328 B.C. during his campaign in Bactria at the foot of the Pamirs (now called Uzbekistan), Alexander the Great and his soldiers reached the foot of a cliff whose approaches were dominated by a fortress. The king of the country had entrenched himself in this fortress.

Alexander demanded that King Oxyartes surrender his arms in return for safe conduct. The king laughed. He was surrounded by brave men and had more than enough food and water to withstand a long siege. Besides, as far as he was concerned, the fortress was impregnable. No man could ever scale the vertical cliff face. Alexander should return with his soldiers once they had grown wings.

Johann Gustav Droysen, in his biography of Alexander, writes: "Determined that the fortress should be taken at all costs, Alexander had the herald proclaim throughout his camp that a second cliff towering above the fortress must be climbed and that the first twelve to do this would be richly rewarded. Three hundred Macedonians, all skilled mountaineers, stepped forward and received their orders. Each was

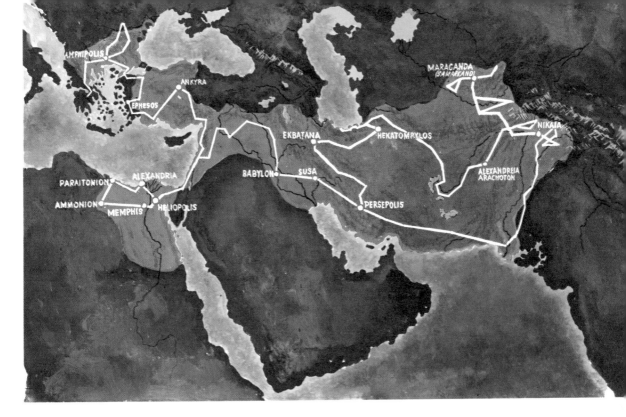

equipped with strong ropes and iron pegs similar to those used in securing the tents. At midnight they approached the steepest part of the cliff, which was, consequently, the least likely to be guarded. They soon began their struggle against the slippery ice surface and the loose snow and rock which came hurtling down at them; with every step the problems increased and the danger grew. Thirty of these daring men plunged into the abyss below, but, eventually, at daybreak, those remaining had reached the top. Once there, they waved their white capes. As soon as he saw this pre-arranged signal Alexander again sent out a messenger, who informed the enemy's advance posts that Alexander had found his winged soldiers and that they were, at that moment, in position above the enemy's heads. Any further resistance was impossible."

The storming of this fortress was not the only mountaineering feat of Alexander's soldiers, however. They traversed the Taurus and then the Hindu Kush mountains in winter (the latter at a height of 10,000 feet!) and pushed on to the Himalayas. Did Alexander really want to found a great empire stretching from the east to the west? Or was his

The campaigns of Alexander the Great.

After the Romans had conquered the Alps they began to open routes through them. A Roman road at Bons in the French Alps. The grooves were cut into the rock to prevent the carts from skidding.

An explosion on the Lagazoni in autumn 1917.

Soldiers washing their clothes at the "Ice-town" in the Marmolada glacier.

purpose to find out where the end of the Earth was? Whatever the reasons, Alexander went no further than the Himalayas.

The fight for the Rote Wand

The hardest-ever mountain fighting took place more recently—during World War I between Italian and Austrian troops. More than two-thirds of the front in this struggle lay at a height of over 6,500 feet amidst rock and ice. The highest gun emplacement was on the summit of Mount Ortles at a height of 12,792 feet. When the soldiers ran out of bullets they fought on with stones, man to man. On the other hand, there was also much material expenditure along this front. The Italians, for example, bored a tunnel 1,180 yards long under the Lagazoni Mountain so that they could blow up the Austrians at the top of the mountain with 70,000 pounds of explosives. The Austrians built a tunnel almost six miles long inside one of the glaciers on the Marmolada mountain, and in it they constructed a real town in the ice. During icy winter storms the soldiers had to remain at their posts, in spite of 40 degrees of frost. The most dangerous enemy for both sides, however, was the avalanche. On one occasion a valley in the Dolomites was buried in a barrage of snow from all sides, and the Austrians and Italians were both forced to seek shelter in the only safe spot available. The hostility between the two groups was quickly forgotten, however, as both sides set about rescuing their trapped comrades from the common enemy.

But the fighting was also very dogged. The battle for one mountain alone, the Rotè Wand, lasted twenty-nine months. Soon after the outbreak of the war, when the Italians had occupied all the prominent peaks above the town of Sesto, the Austrians were still able to establish a position at the last minute on the 9,636-foot Rote Wand.

It was a fight waged not only with rifles and artillery. It was also a struggle against overhanging rock and steep ice-falls. A battle was begun in wild, mountainous terrain

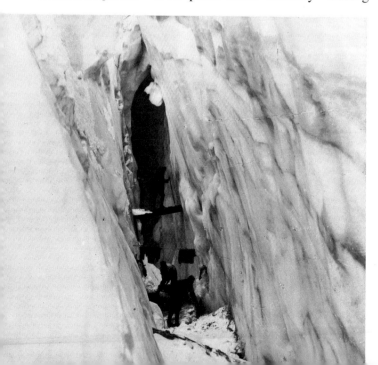

where today mountaineers are only to be found equipped with protective helmets, ropes and ice-axes. It was a war in which men not only shot at one another, but in which they also climbed against one another. From the Italian high command the prominent climber, Italo Lunelli, was appointed leader of the assault on the Rote Wand. He had in his command a special troop of 120 men, who were divided into four units; the *arrampicatori*, who were to be the first to climb the rock face; the *legatori*, who could then secure the ropes; the *scalatori*, who would afterwards fix up rope ladders and

The World War I fighting stations in the Dolomites have since become a great tourist attraction.

wooden ladders; and the *portatori*, who were to take care of the fresh supplies and equipment.

On the Rote Wand there was no victor or vanquished. In the autumn of 1917 the emphasis of the war suddenly shifted elsewhere, to the Isonzo River. At a stroke the mountain had lost its significance and Italians and Austrians alike abandoned their positions. One of the fighters for the Rote Wand wrote of his departure: "An oppressive, almost unreal silence now lies over the mountain, as if it had become bewitched. . . ." So, peace returned to the Rote Wand.

The 3,575-foot-long Lagazoni Tunnel was restored a few years ago and is today accessible once more with the help of torchlight. Above: *The entrance.*

On the walls of the Dolomites there still remain mouldy old wooden ladders left over from the fighting of more than half a century ago.

CHAPTER 3

THE BIRTH OF ALPINISM

The christening of a mountain

Mont Aiguille (6,815 feet) is a gigantic tower of rock in the French Alps some thirty miles south of Grenoble. On all sides the walls of the tower rise vertically for 900 feet, which explains why, in all old documents, it is referred to as Mons Inaccessibilis—the unclimbable mountain.

In 1492 Columbus sailed to America. In the same year, at the request of King Charles VIII of France, Antoine de Ville and twelve companions (who included a royal ladder-maker and two priests) climbed the Mons Inaccessibilis. At the summit where, amazingly, there is a large fertile meadow, Antoine de Ville set up three crosses, read mass and then—unique in alpine history —christened the mountain! Afterwards de Ville sat down and wrote a precise account of the ascent. In it he concludes: "This is the most terrible, most frightening venture I, or any of our party, have ever undertaken."

A messenger had to deliver the report to the council in Grenoble. Antoine de Ville would only leave the summit when an agent of the king had confirmed his ascent of the mountain. He waited a week before an envoy of the king arrived. The envoy, Ive Levy, saw the tower of rock and wrote in his report: "The very sight of the mountain alone is enough to fill anyone with terror." Antoine de Ville sent the envoy a friendly invitation to join him on the summit. The latter refused the invitation, however, because "he did not wish to provoke God".

Where and how did de Ville climb?

We know that, before 1492, men had already climbed mountains and that, furthermore, they had made some very difficult ascents, but never before de Ville had anyone conquered a rock face of such height and difficulty. For the walls of Mont Aiguille are formidably steep on every side, north, south, east and west.

The question of where Antoine de Ville and his party made their ascent still remains a much discussed mystery even today. The envoy's account, which tells of ladders fixed in sheer walls, is taken far too literally by many alpine historians. They forget that to non-climbers even a steep ravine seems like a sheer cliff face, and that it is very easy to exaggerate.

In the search for de Ville's mysterious ascent route one must take into account the fact that, in the past, mountaineers avoided open rock faces and preferred instead to use ravines to facilitate their ascent. On

Mont Blanc from the north.

ladder provided by the royal ladder-maker, though it would have had to have been at least thirty feet long. A wooden ladder of that length is extremely heavy and it would certainly have called for the labour of at least a dozen men to surmount the cliffs.

And, between these Jacob's ladders balanced against the mountain-side, the less formidable stretches still held many dangers for the climbers. Their every step was a matter of life and death, particularly in those days when boots had smooth leather soles ill-suited for gripping the footholds.

Those first men to climb Mont Aiguille were ignorant of the first rule of mountaineering, namely, that one must always have three secure holds before climbing higher or trying for a fresh hold. They knew absolutely nothing of climbing technique and, above all, they had to fight against giddiness. It is amazing to realize the intensity of the feelings experienced by mountaineers in the past, when they looked down into the empty depths below them. Even in the accounts written by moun-

Mont Aiguille.

The first man to ascend Mont Aiguille probably climbed this gully in 1492.

Mont Aiguille there is just such a ravine, cutting deep into the rock face some 600 feet west of the ascent route normally used today, which was first opened up in the years 1878–80 by the French Alpine Club using wire cables. The ravine is dark and precipitous and steep rock faces extend its entire length. It is possible that de Ville could have climbed these rock faces with the help of a

taineers in the 19th century one reads of "horrible, penetrating glances into the deep", whenever they write about some exposed point where, today, even tourists can stand without quaking. 1492 . . . the year Columbus sails to America. 1492 . . . at the request of King Charles VIII of France Antoine de Ville and his twelve companions climb the Mons Inaccessibilis. De Ville was a mercenary, an adventurer like Columbus. Columbus set sail into the wide unknown. Antoine de Ville climbed a hitherto unmapped part of the world and thereby completed an alpine achievement centuries ahead of his time and which was, therefore, extolled by his contemporaries as a miracle.

Why did de Ville undertake the climb?

The climbing of the Mons Inaccessibilis brought the French king neither increased power nor increased wealth. To Antoine de Ville it probably brought gold and it most definitely brought honour. On the other hand, he could quite easily have lost his life in the adventure. If we draw any conclusions from de Ville's own account then it must be that the adventure, in itself, was more precious to him than the gold or the honour.

This delight in adventure is still the chief motivation for mountaineering today. The yearning to experience something beyond our day-to-day existence is a feeling shared by almost everyone. The adventure we see on the cinema or television screens cannot satisfy this yearning, but mountains certainly can. There, anyone can experience real adventure at any time, whether they are seventeen or seventy. "How simple everything becomes in the mountains! Our aims become clear and obvious! There is the mountain

—and here am I. Between dawn and dusk lies the outcome!" So says Oskar Erich Meyer in his famous book about mountains *Deed and Dream.*

The day of the birth of alpinism had dawned—in 1492. And afterwards? Nearly three centuries went by before another man saw in climbing a mountain the great aim of his life.

The summit of Mont Aiguille turns out to be a huge meadow!

It all began with a competition

"Monsieur Horace Benédict de Saussure from Ghent promises a high reward to anyone who can discover an accessible path to the summit of Mont Blanc." In 1760 this notice could be read on the parish notice-board of Chamonix. At that time de Saussure was twenty.

Eighteen years later, after his eighth journey to Mont Blanc, Saussure began to doubt whether it was possible for anyone ever to reach the summit. In 1786, however, Jacques Balmat, a guide and treasure-seeker from Chamonix, and Michel-Gabriel Paccard, the town doctor, eventually reached the summit. It had already been known since 1745 that Mont Blanc was the highest mountain in Europe. Its height is stated as being 15,623–15,633 feet. The range in heights is explained by the fact that the summit of the mountain consists only of snow and ice and, as the temperature varies from season to season, different height measurements are recorded.

It was not until a year later that the man who initiated this first ascent of Mont Blanc, himself stood on the summit of his mountain with Balmat. In the contemporary pictures of this noble scholar Saussure, he appears as a rococo gentleman with a pigtail and a friendly disposition towards life. In fact he was a fanatic for whom the conquering of Mont Blanc had become an obsession. Now that he had at last reached the summit he stamped his feet violently in the snow, not out of joy but out of anger that the mountain had thwarted him for so long. He now began his scientific work which lasted four and a half hours. Saussure worked with a barometer, thermometer, hygrometer and electrometer; he boiled water, fired a pistol, measured the pulse rate of his companion and compared the colour of

Horace-Benédict de Saussure.

the sky with colour samples he had taken with him.

Saussure would probably never have reached the summit of Mont Blanc if it had not been for Jacques Balmat. In the contemporary pictures of Balmat he appears as a somewhat shy man. A dreamer? He was certainly that too. On the day he became the first man ever to stand on the summit of Mont Blanc his eighteen-days-old son died. He was honoured for his ascent of Mont Blanc but, as he grew older, he returned to the life he had known as a

young man—the life of a treasure hunter. At the age of seventy-two he fell to his death while searching for a mysterious gold-mine in a deep ravine. His body was never found. The site of Saussure's grave also remains unknown.

Snowblind and sunburnt faces

Balmat and Dr Paccard arrived back in Chamonix after their first ascent of Mont Blanc. A year later Saussure issued his twenty-man expedition with dark veils to protect them against the snow and, thereafter, no one was snowblind or sunburnt again. Knowledge had been won through experience.

Balmat and Paccard had climbed Mont Blanc without ropes, ice-axes, crampons, fur-lined jackets, bivouac equipment, sunburn cream or snow goggles. They climbed in their everyday clothes and their only equipment consisted of long staffs, with which they helped one another across crevasses often more than 90 feet deep. In this way they climbed higher into unmapped regions of the

Full of crevasses and fissures, the Bossons Glacier was crossed by the man who was also first to climb Mont Blanc.

world, where unknown danger lay in waiting for them.

All previous climbers to attempt the great height which Balmat and Paccard reached had been injured. Palpitation of the heart and restricted breathing, nose-bleeds and complete exhaustion were the major

fought for more than a quarter of a century to conquer his mountain and his fight was followed with interest by educated people. The victory of this aristocrat and scholar over the mountain made mountaineering socially acceptable in Europe. At that time also the concept of alpin-

Opposite: A mountaineer on a glacier at the beginning of the 19th century. There were no rucksacks then, and provisions and covering for a bivouac had to be carried in baskets.

On Mont Blanc there is no cross or sign to mark the summit — only snow and ice.

problems they encountered. It was popularly believed in Chamonix at that time that nobody could survive even a few minutes on the summit of Mont Blanc. In spite of this Balmat and Paccard dared to push forward into the death-zone.

After the ascent of the highest mountain in the Alps, mountaineering gained a more up-to-date image. All previous climbs in the Alps (for example the ascent of Mont Ventoux (6,216 feet) in 1336 by the Italian writer Francesco Petrarca, or the ascent of Mount Pilatus (6,932 feet) in 1555 by the Swiss scholar Konrad Gesner) had been spontaneous ideas, mere week-end excursions. The conquest of Mont Aiguille had been an extraordinary event, but nevertheless it was still only a local one. Saussure, however,

A night descent of Mont Blanc. An exaggerated representation by the Englishman J. D. H. Browne drawn in 1853.

33

ism was born; a term now used to describe all types of mountaineering on all the world's mountains.

The first woman on the summit of Mont Blanc...

was Marie Paradis from Chamonix. She was persuaded to go along by the guides who, like the advertising men of our own time, realized as early as 1809 that a woman would provide effective publicity for their venture. Marie says: ". . . on the grand plateau I could go no further, I was very ill and I lay down on the snow. But I was seized and pushed and pulled until we finally got to the top. I couldn't see, I couldn't breathe, I couldn't speak. . . ."

... and the first fatalities!

20th August 1820. . . . The Russian naturalist, Dr Joseph Hamel, climbs towards the summit of Mont Blanc accompanied by two English scholars and a dozen guides. Before the last push to the summit the party stops once more for a rest. Hamel writes a note: "Arrived at the summit of Mont Blanc at . . ." The exact time of arrival was to be filled in on the summit. A carrier-

A bivouac at 11,633 feet on the steep southern flank of Mont Blanc. The small hut, offering accommodation for five people, was erected as a base for an attempt on the difficult Peuterey Ridge.

The prussiker knot can easily be slid along when slack but otherwise remains quite secure. A fallen climber can work his way up by putting his weight on one sling and sliding the other up the rope.

Policemen and game wardens in Africa's national parks are made familiar with the prussiker knot. This is an essential part of their training in mountain rescue.

A two-man roped party on a snow-covered glacier. Secured to his comrade by rope, the man in front tests the ground for crevasses.

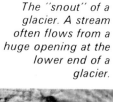

The "snout" of a glacier. A stream often flows from a huge opening at the lower end of a glacier.

pigeon which had been taken with them would then fly down into the valley with the news.

They climb on . . . and then suddenly the whole snow-slope begins to move . . . and drags the party with it down into the depths! The avalanche comes to a standstill while human figures—pale as ghosts—clamber out of the snow. Stunned, they grope their way towards one another, but three of the guides fail to rise from their white graves . . . they are the first to die on Mont Blanc. 15th August 1861 . . . in the churchyard in Chamonix a sack is emptied of its gruesome contents—the remains of the three men who were swallowed up by the glacier forty-one years before and carried

along by it to its journey's end. The former guide Couttet, now over seventy years old, recognized amongst the remains the almost undamaged hand of an old friend—another of the guides.

Today we can drive through Mont Blanc. The journey through the tunnel from Chamonix on the French side to Courmayeur on the Italian lasts about forty minutes. It is also possible to cross the mountain by cable-car. The cable-car (Chamonix–Aiguille du Midi–Turinerhütte–Entrèves) which is regarded as a new wonder of the world, travels at a height of almost 12,000 feet above the Mont Blanc plateau. The summit proper is still, however, the preserve of mountaineers only.

Is Mont Blanc a dangerous mountain?

Today there exist fifty ascent routes all of varying grades of difficulty. The easiest route leads first of all over a wide crevasse-torn glacier, then over a narrow ice-ridge to the summit. For an experienced mountaineer, used to high climbs and equipped with ice-axe, rope and crampons, an ascent of Mont Blanc is a very strenuous, but technically uncomplicated climb . . . if the weather is good. The white cap of the mountain is not always surrounded by blue skies. The sudden changes in weather are feared by mountaineers. Already many have become disoriented in mists and snowstorms, or have fallen victims to snow-covered crevasses or avalanches, or they have frozen to death at the height of summer in the winter cold of a bivouac. Every year there are some victims on Mont Blanc in spite of the availability of modern equipment and the most modern methods of rescue from the air!

Mist on a cornice demands the greatest concentration from every mountaineer. Many climbers have had fatal accidents caused by the collapse of a cornice.

CHAPTER 4

THE FIGHT FOR THE MATTERHORN

The "Golden Age" of alpinism

The conquest of Mont Blanc was the beginning, Saussure was the pioneer. The conquest of the Alps had begun.

In 1788, that is one year after Saussure's ascent of Mont Blanc, the French scholar Déodat de Dolomieu was travelling in the region south of the Brenner Pass, when he discovered strangely shaped pinnacles and towers formed from rock hitherto unknown to the world of science. Later, the rock was named after him. He had discovered the Dolomites. In 1800 an expedition over the Grossglockner (12,340 feet) led by Prince Salm-Reifferschied, a cardinal and the prince-bishop of Gurk, ended in victory.

But it was no cardinal or prince-bishop, only a simple priest called Giuseppe Terza, who two years later lost his life in an attempt to climb the Marmolada. Even a member of the Austrian imperial family, Archduke Johann, only narrowly escaped death in an avalanche during an attempt to conquer the Grossvenediger in 1828. However paradoxical it may sound, it still remains a fact that the first alpinists were totally unaware that mountaineering could be dangerous, because they still had no experience at that time and, therefore, recognized absolutely none of the dangers.

By the middle of the 19th century a hundred of the larger alpine peaks —such as Ortles, the Jungfrau and the Zugspitze—had already been climbed for the first time. "Will our grandsons succeed in the future in conquering the last of all the alpine peaks?" was the question posed by one worried alpinist in 1854. But he did not know at the time that in that very year the "Golden Age" of alpinism was about to begin.

This "Golden Age" of alpinism remains even today an inexplicable phenomenon to all alpine historians. Suddenly—as if on cue—there followed a mass invasion by English mountaineers of the western regions of the Alps. A mountain fever seemed to have broken out, and the Alps became the "Playground of Europe" (to use the phrase coined by the Englishman, Leslie Stephen). One unclimbed mountain after another fell to this new onslaught and in a single decade several hundred first climbs were made. Eventually this fever also gripped the inhabitants of the Continent, and in the course of the next ten years it was principally the eastern regions which became the target of assaults on peaks. This fascinating "Golden Age" only lasted two decades, but, by the end of it, nearly all the important peaks had been conquered.

Of all the many mountains only

The Matterhorn.

one had offered its conquerors any serious resistance, and this was the most beautiful and most challenging of them all—the Matterhorn.

Whymper and Carrel

Let us look first at the Englishman, Edward Whymper. Until 1860 this young engraver had never seen a mountain, nor even climbed a hill. In 1860, aged twenty, he was travelling in the Alps to make sketches of some big mountain peaks on behalf of a publishing firm. In the summer of 1861 Whymper saw the Matterhorn for the first time, and he immediately made an attempt to climb it, which all the best mountaineers of the time claimed was impossible. Whymper's attempt ended in defeat. But this defeat merely increased his resolve "to return with a companion and besiege the mountain for so long that either it or we will be beaten".

Now let us look at the Italian, Jean Carrel, who was born in the shadow of the Matterhorn. As early as 1857 he had attempted to climb the mountain with his brother, and the mountaineer Abbé Aimé Gorret. In 1857 Whymper did not even know that the Matterhorn existed. Carrel believed right from the beginning that he would be the first person to stand on the summit. It seemed obvious that any further attempts to climb the mountain by either Whymper or Carrel would be undertaken together.

Whymper set his imagination to work on devising the best possible equipment for the coming struggle. For the nights spent bivouacking he constructed a portable moun-

A mid-19th century mountaineer. The leader, on the left, is carrying the rope (and what a poor rope it is!) very casually. Here is a clear illustration of how much alpine technique and equipment have developed during the last 100 years.

taineer's tent, and to overcome the problem of sheer rock faces he constructed a kind of grappling-iron. In 1863 he began his journey and among his luggage he even had two collapsible ladders.

14th July 1865

At last, in the summer of 1865, the conditions on the Matterhorn were at their most favourable for an assault. Whymper and Carrel had already discovered that the best ascent route to the summit was on the Italian Ridge. But, when Whymper arrived to prepare for the assault, he was to learn that Carrel had already agreed to make the ascent with some Italians. Whymper and Carrel had become rivals.

Whymper reached the summit of the Matterhorn with his companions on 14th July. On the same day Carrel and his party were themselves only 300 feet below the summit on the Italian side. On the descent from the summit a climber from the triumphant party slipped and pulled three of his companions with him. The rope snapped and four of the seven first men to climb the Matterhorn plunged down into the abyss. . . . "For a few seconds we watched our unfortunate companions tumble down the slope, fighting with outstretched hands for some kind of finger-hold. They were still unhurt as one by one they disappeared from view and crashed from cliff to cliff down a drop of almost 4,000 feet", Whymper later related. He and his companions had made a mistake that had already cost the lives of many mountaineers: during the descent, they had allowed the joy of success or their extreme fatigue to affect their concentration.

Whymper's intention to "besiege the mountain for so long that either it or we will be beaten" had taken on a grimly real meaning. He left the

Edward Whymper at the age of 25.

Louis Trenker as Carrel in The Fight for the Matterhorn.

Falling rocks on the Matterhorn. A drawing by Edward Whymper.

Matterhorn both as victor and as vanquished.

Mountains had taken their toll before the Matterhorn catastrophe; but mountaineering was, nevertheless, not considered dangerous. The disaster was discussed in newspapers and magazines, and, henceforth, every mountaineer was considered a potential suicide and a candidate for certain death.

The Angels of the Mountains

Clearly, as the number of mountaineers rose, so too did the number of fatalities. And an accident on a mountain is always a terrible event, even if there are no deaths. How is one to bring someone with a broken foot down a steep cliff face or down a badly fissured glacier into the valley. At one time he had to be carried. Yet anyone, who has not performed that action himself, cannot imagine just how much strength it calls for, to climb or to make one's way through a field of boulders when carrying a man who is groaning with agony.

In March 1896 an avalanche buried three mountaineers on the Raxalpe near Vienna. One of them was the brother of the well known alpinist Heinrich Pfannl. This disaster led to the founding of an alpine rescue commission that provided the first mountain rescue service in the world. Until that time, rescue operations had been conducted by the companions of the victims or by mountain guides, or even by a quickly assembled party of strong men (who, while not lacking in spirit, had no knowledge of mountaineering). Today the primitive equipment and rescue methods employed by the early rescue teams would certainly arouse a sympathetic smile from their modern counterparts. But it was the

pioneers' example that set the pattern, and ever since people have continuously worked to improve equipment and methods. Today, anyone who gets into difficulties on a mountain, and whose distress call is heard, can almost always depend on being brought to safety.

The alpine distress call is six signals per minute, then a minute's interval, followed by another six signals. They can be by sound (shouting, whistling) or visual (waving, flashing).

A fall which fortunately did not prove fatal. The second man was able to hold his companion by the rope.

Opposite: Fall on the Matterhorn *by Gustave Doré, 1869.*

43

The Angels of the Mountains float down in their helicopters to the victims or dangle over cliff and ice on thin steel cables hundreds of feet long. They are equipped with adjustable stretcher-sledges and communicate with one another by means of walkie-talkies. The training of a good mountain rescuer today takes at least a year. He is not just a highly skilled mountaineer, but must have the technical ability to manipulate the complex equipment with confident precision, and, furthermore the medical knowledge that would be required should the injured be in need of first aid.

It is always reassuring to know that the mountain rescue service exists. But no one should rely on it, to the point of undertaking a climb that is beyond his capabilities. The statement of a well known mountaineer is as relevant as ever: "The greatest skill in mountaineering is the ability to practise it and grow old."

In July 1965 at the foot of the Matterhorn there took place a great festival: the hundredth anniversary of the first ascent was being celebrated.

Guests from all over the world were invited to take part and more than 600 people took up the invitation. The Swiss postal service issued a special stamp. Eight tons of television equipment were transported to the foot of the Swiss side of the ridge in order to be able to televise a commemorative ascent of the Matterhorn.

With the help of apparatus using steel cables, it is now possible to conduct recovery operations from even the most difficult cliffs. The apparatus even allows a cable-lift to be set up to transport the injured climber as quickly and as comfortably as possible.

CHAPTER 5

HIGHER STILL
HIGHER

Popocatepetl

In 1519 the Spaniard Cortez landed with a small company of soldiers on the Mexican coast and began the pillage of the Aztec empire.

At the same time, the 17,000-foot volcano Popocatepetl (Smoking Mountain) began again to spew forth fire after 200 years of lying dormant. The Aztecs took this as an evil omen. One of Cortez' men Lieutenant Diego de Ordaz wanted to climb the fiery mountain with some of his men, in order to prove to the Aztecs that the Christian God was stronger than their idols. The column of smoke from Popocatepetl rose high into the sky. As far as the natives at its foot were concerned every member of the small expedition was doomed to die.

The higher the men penetrated, the louder the mountain's rumblings sounded in their ears. The bearers refused to go a step farther, but the Spaniards trudged on—on through steep snowfields and lava flows, often forced to crawl on all fours. The sulphur fumes oppressed their lungs. Sheer fatigue. That scarcely resistible longing to lie down and sleep.

Defeated, beaten back by the mountain, the Spaniards were, in the end, overjoyed to regain the valley alive. Cortez, however, had it announced that his men had reached the summit. The idols could not be seen to be stronger than the God of the Christians.

This defeat, nevertheless, preyed on Cortez' mind. So, having slaughtered the ruling Aztec class in a gruesome blood-bath, he gave the command that the very last symbol of their resistance be crushed. He ordered that Popocatepetl be climbed. By now the volcano was no longer active.

The order was carried out by Franciscos Montano, and right up until the discovery of the Inca temples on Cerro Gallan in 1955, the ascent made by his party was considered to represent a new world record in successful summit climbs. Franciscos' real achievement, however, was that the containers of sulphur that he brought back from the volcanic crater at Popocatepetl's summit made possible the manufacture of gunpowder.

Mountain sickness

The phenomenon, which had affected de Ordaz and his men, was first recognized in 1590 by a Spanish missionary priest, José de Acosta, on his crossing of the Andes. Feelings of weakness and bouts of giddiness, extreme lethargy and headaches, anxiety and shortness of breath—all these changes, experienced by a person at great heights, were attributed by the

Popocatepetl.

The following labels appear on the drawing: Spitze des Chimborazo, Höhe des Popocatepetl, Höhe des Pic de Teyde, Spitze des Cotopaxi, Höhe des Montblanc, Höhe des Vesuv.

A drawing of Chimborazo made in 1808 by Alexander von Humboldt. It depicts the summits of Chimborazo, Cotopaxi, Popocatepetl, Mont Blanc, Pic de Teyde and Vesuvius.

perceptive priest to the thinner air of the mountains.

Today we know that the cause of mountain sickness can be traced to the reduction in the oxygen supply to the bloodstream when at an increased altitude; in consequence, the body's tissues receive less oxygen and disturbances occur in the metabolic and nervous systems. It is interesting to note that the human organism is capable of adjusting to this stress relatively quickly. In other words it is possible for a person unaccustomed to high altitudes to suffer from mountain sickness at an altitude of 6,500 feet, whilst a highly trained member of a mountaineering expedition will still be unaffected by it at 23,000 feet.

As a group of present-day researchers were approaching the research station on the Jungfraujoch (11,200 feet) in the high Alps in order to conduct some scientific experiments on mountain sickness, they found themselves experiencing the phenomenon at first hand. "The light-headedness produced by the altitude so overcame us, that we broke into uncontrollable fits of laughter at every triviality, sat down on the cases and then made remarkably clumsy attempts to unpack these. Later we had to develop various methods of testing—a procedure which, at low altitudes, we had followed on innumerable occasions. Convinced of the correctness of our procedural technique, we managed to patch together a completely false system of tests. In consequence the first few days' measurements recorded some most startling effects of altitude, which on later examination revealed themselves to be rather a result of the altitude's influence on our thought processes."

The Watchtower of the World

From the mid-18th century all geographers were agreed that Chimborazo in the South American Andes was the highest mountain in the world—at 20,600 feet.

The first attempt to climb this mountain, also known as the Watch-

tower of the World, took place about 1740. Charles Marie de Lacondamine and Pierre Bouguer, members of a French geodetic expedition, reached a height of about 15,500 feet.

In 1802 the German natural scientist Alexander von Humboldt and a few companions attempted to climb Chimborazo. According to the scientist's calculations, they reached a height of 19,113 feet. Critics later discovered a mistake in Humboldt's calculations and reduced the achieved height to about 17,500 feet (that is to say approximately 350 feet less than Popocatepetl's height). The great scientist died before this discovery was made and so was able to live happily on in the belief, that of all mortals he was the one who had climbed highest in the world.

In 1831 the French scientist Jean Baptiste Boussingault and his party reportedly attained a height of 19,500 feet. Boussingault had an original formula for countering mountain sickness—complete

silence whilst climbing, communication solely by means of sign language and even during rest periods use of only whispered words. He later asserted that it was only as a result of these tough measures that his expedition was able to reach such a great height.

Chimborazo was in fact first climbed in 1880 by Edward Whymper, the conqueror of the Matterhorn and his great rival from those days, the alpine guide Jean Antoine Carrel. Fifteen years had passed since the struggle for the Matterhorn and the two men had become friends instead of rivals. After their return to the valley, doubts were expressed as to whether Whymper and Carrel really had reached the summit. The conqueror of the Matterhorn, at that time already over forty years old, was still fired by the same youthful spirit. He wanted to put an end to this suspicion. Together with two natives, he again made the ascent. At the summit he obtained a written affidavit to this effect and on his return to the

Chimborazo.

valley had this affidavit legally ratified.

The first ascent of Chimborazo. A drawing by Edward Whymper.

"I have discovered the highest mountain in the world!"

For about seventy-five years Chim-

The Himalayas with Mount Everest seen from a plane.

borazo was considered to be the highest mountain in the world. Up until the beginning of the 19th century Western geographers were almost wholly ignorant of the 1500-mile-long principal chain of the Himalayas. It was not known that, even from the very earliest times, people there had been crossing passes more than 16,000 feet high. True, as early as the 17th and 18th centuries Jesuit priests had brought back from their missionary journeys between India and Tibet reports of "high mountains", but the concept "high" is well known to be relative, and is scarcely a reliable guide.

The British Survey officer, Captain Gerard, was the first to produce concrete figures: the lower Himalayas all have a height of between 16,000 and 19,000 feet. What was sensational about the survey work, that he undertook in the years between 1817 and 1821, was the discovery of a mountain for which a height of 26,525 feet was recorded— Mount Dhaulagiri (according to present-day measurements 26,810 feet).

And then in 1852—as tradition has it—one of the officials at the Topographical Institute (Survey of India) burst into his superior's office and reported excitedly: "Sir, I've found the highest mountain in the world!"

During 1849 and 1850, one particular peak, situated about 150 miles from India's plains had been surveyed from six different positions and analysis of the data had produced a reading of approximately 28,730 feet. The point that had previously been known as Summit XV was named after the founder of the Survey of India, Sir George Everest.

Just how high the highest mountain in the world actually is will never be determined for certain. Consider that the snow cover on the summit varies from year to year, that it is possible that the measured height of the survey position itself is slightly inaccurate, even that further mistakes may arise through faults in the theodolites or as a consequence of light refractions. After the Assam earthquake of 1950, Mount Everest's summit is supposed to have been lifted almost 200 feet higher. Indeed the Himalayan peaks as a whole are supposed to have risen about 5,000–6,000 feet since the end of the last Ice Age and are continuing to rise by about four inches a year.

In 1944 it was believed that a peak

A "foothill" of Mount Everest—the 25,429-foot Nuptse.

One of the great Himalayan explorers was the Swede Sven Hedin. His journey in the winter of 1906/7 took him over a 19,374-foot pass. This illustration is from his famous book Transhimalaya.

in excess of 29,000 feet had been discovered. During World War II, an American air pilot broke through the cloud cover and, with his altimeter indicating a height of 32,000 feet, observed at his side a white wall, the tip of which towered high over his plane. The war was still on but, nevertheless, the news of his sensational discovery of what was, in fact, "the highest mountain in the world", flashed across the whole world. The mountain was climbed for the first time in 1960 by a Chinese expedition. Its height: a mere 23,280 feet. The American pilot's altimeter had been faulty.

Two mountains vanish

The first attempt to find a path up the highest mountain in the world was made as early as 1921. The British were determined to be the first to climb the mountain that they had discovered. But first they had to find a route to the mountain itself. It meant pushing forward into rugged, unknown territory. What was only 100 miles by air represented in practice a march of about 300 miles. One member of this expedition died of exhaustion on the march. At last, the foot of the mountain was reached. By what route could it best be climbed? From advances to a height of 23,000 feet the expedition returned with the conclusion: Mount Everest can indeed be climbed! . . . and, furthermore, it is now known by what approach route! 1922 . . . a snowstorm ended all further attempts. Greatest height achieved: 27,000 feet. The mountain had claimed seven victims. 1924 . . . this time the summit itself was to be conquered. Just as it is only possible to climb a ladder by means of the rungs, so, too, on a mountain of over 26,000 feet, camps have to be established after every

day's march. Small tents are pitched in positions safe from avalanches, tents in which provisions, oxygen cylinders, medicaments, sleeping-bags, etc., are stored.

The highest camp established by the British in 1924 was at 26,440 feet. From there, on 8th June, Andrew Irvine (twenty-two) and George H. Leigh-Mallory (thirty-seven) set out on their assault on the summit. Mallory was the strongest man of the expedition, both in body and mind. He was also the most familiar with the mountain: he had been there in 1921, when the shortest approved route was discovered. In 1922 he had reached a height of 27,000 feet; in 1924 he had been

mainly responsible for the setting up of the advance camp. Lieutenant-Colonel E. F. Norton, who had reached a height of 27,878 feet on this expedition, says of Mallory: "An indefatigable spirit enabled him to overcome all weaknesses. He drew on such reserves of will power that one could never say for sure whether he was tired or not. He pursued the conquest of Everest with a single-mindedness that bordered on religious fanaticism."

On this eighth day of June 1924, the geologist N. E. Odell was climbing alone from Camp V to Camp VI with a rucksack of provisions. At about 25,500 feet the mists thinned and Odell saw Mallory

Ama Dablam (22,232 feet), one of the most beautifully formed mountains in the Himalayas.

George H. Leigh-Mallory. The cross on the sketch marks the point on Mount Everest where Mallory and Irvine were last seen — Camp VI at 26,440 feet.

and Irvine. . . . "On a snowfield beneath the last stage but one before the summit-cone, I noticed a black speck nearing the cliff-shelf. A second followed. . . ." Then the mists closed in again. The two figures disappeared in the clouds. At 2 p.m. Odell reached Camp VI and deposited the provisions. It had begun to snow. Odell took shelter in the tent. At about 4 p.m. the blizzard had passed. The summit was again visible. No one was to be seen. As there was only room for two people at Camp VI Odell again descended to Camp IV to leave the two advance camps available for the conquerors of Everest. It was a clear night and he continually gazed back up the mountain, looking for a light-signal. But on the slopes of the great mountain there was only the weak glimmer of the moonlight, reflected from the snow-covered summits. Odell hoped that it would light the homeward path of those two lonely men up there.

9th June . . . as soon as day dawned people focused their field glasses on Camp VI. There was nothing to be seen. Towards midday Odell and two Sherpas ascended to Camp V. They reached it in the midst of a raging storm and spent the night there. 10th June . . . the two Sherpas were suffering from mountain sickness. Odell made his way up to Camp VI alone. The tent was untouched. Mallory and Irvine had not returned. Odell knew that they would now never return. Never. Yet, for a few hours he tried to find at least some sign of them. He found nothing. He was the last person to have seen Mallory and Irvine alive. In the vicinity of the summit. . . .

Had the two mountaineers reached the summit? And how did they come to die? Through exhaustion, frozen to death? Did they fall to their death? Did they die before or after reaching the summit? That is a mystery of Mount Everest and will never be solved. The general opinion is that Mallory and Irvine probably never reached the summit.

Hillary and Tenzing break camp to begin their assault on the highest mountain in the world.

The conquest of the highest mountain in the world

On 29th May 1953, a British expedition, led by Sir John Hunt, ended a struggle that had lasted more than thirty years.

Hillary and Tenzing stayed on the summit for a quarter of an hour. Hillary photographed Tenzing, who had fastened the pennants of the three participating nations, Great Britain, Nepal and India, to his ice-axe. Tenzing dug a small hole in the snow in which he placed chocolate, a packet of biscuits and a handful of sugar—offerings to the gods, who, according to the beliefs of pious Buddhists, inhabit the summit. Hillary also dug a hole in the snow, and in it put a small cross which two days previously the leader of the expedition had given to him for his arrival at the summit.

Since that day Everest has been climbed several times. 1971 saw the start of the biggest Himalayan expedition yet: twenty-eight top-class mountaineers from twelve different countries took with them 36 tons of equipment, and the main goal of the expedition was to master the 8,100-foot south-west face of Mount Everest. Yet, even with the participation of the world's leading mountaineers, using the most up-to-date equipment available, the expedition failed to reach the summit.

This failure did not, however, deter the 1972 Anglo-German expedition to Everest.

The base camp on Mount Everest of the ill-fated 1971 International Himalayan Expedition.

CHAPTER 6

THE FIGHT FOR THE
26,000-FOOT PEAKS

The death-zone

In mountaineering the term "death-zone" is used to refer to heights of over 26,000 feet. When in 1875 two men died after their balloon had reached a height of 27,600 feet, it was concluded that death was inevitable at such a height. Prince Luigi Amedeo of Savoy, Duke of the Abruzzi, set out in 1909 on an expedition to the Himalayas, with the aim of determining what height man could in fact reach. The first achievement of the expedition was to break the world climbing record by reaching 24,368 feet on Mount Chogolisa (previously known as Broad Peak). However, the most celebrated success of the expedition was that it established that man can survive in the highest regions of the Earth, over an extended period of time, without detriment to his health. An optimistic, but mistaken conclusion. For 24,368 feet is considerably less than 26,000 feet—and it is at this height, that man enters the death-zone. The shortage of oxygen, the reduced flow of blood to the brain have far-reaching effects on even the toughest and most experienced of mountaineers.

In 1933 the Englishman Francis Smythe, standing on Mount Everest at about 28,000 feet, suddenly observed two kites floating across the sky: "My brain seemed to be functioning normally and I deliberately put myself to the test by looking away. The objects did not stay in my field of view, but they were still there when I looked back." Smythe, who was climbing alone, also experienced the feeling of being roped to a companion. Later, when he was about to eat a biscuit, he stopped to break it in two to give a piece to his comrade. On turning round he was stunned to see that he was in fact alone.

Since then many mountaineers have brought back accounts of an invisible companion in the death-zone. One who did so was Reinhold Messner, who, together with his brother Gunther, successfully crossed Nanga Parbat (26,660 feet).

Reinhold Messner, an uncomplicated modern young man, recounts: "Suddenly a third person was there, climbing steadily, a bit to my right . . . a few yards away from me . . . then just out of sight. I was sure that there was someone there. I felt his presence. Some noise or other seemed to be proof of the fact. He didn't speak. He was simply there. . . ."

The scientific explanation for these ghostly apparitions has, so far, been that they were just hallucinations. But the accounts of the world's best mountaineers have at least made one thing clear. No one can survive extended periods in the

The very first thing to be done when climbing a 26,000-foot peak is to secure an ascent route to the high-lying camps, using fixed ropes, bridges and hanging ladders.

A mountaineer on an expedition is above all a beast of burden.

The photographs (below and right) were taken during the first high performance test in alpine history, in the winter of 1969 in the Bernese Oberland. The experiment was designed to test the reaction of the human body to extreme conditions at high altitudes.

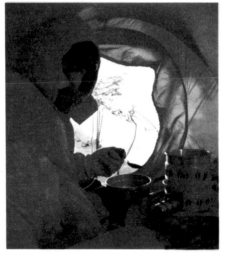

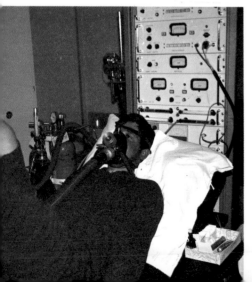

death-zone without harmful effects. Breathing apparatus is of no assistance in this case.

Breathing equipment was used by the very first expedition to Mount Everest, equipment weighing about 381 pounds a piece! Since then the weight has been reduced, but it still represents a heavy burden for a man who has to climb or cut steps in the ice, especially considering the other items he has to carry—the alpine equipment, the protective layers of clothing, the food and the drink (at such heights the need for liquid nourishment is enormous).

As early as 1922 an altitude of 26,731 feet was reached on Mount Everest without breathing apparatus, and several other mountains of over 26,000 feet have been climbed without its aid. Up to a certain altitude, and for a certain length of time, it is possible to acclimatize the human organism. But, in spite of acclimatization, in spite of physical fitness, and in spite of the most up-to-date breathing apparatus, it is uncanny just how quickly a man's resources are used up at altitudes over 26,000 feet; life burns away as certainly as a candle.

The terrors of the monsoon and the good men of the Himalayas

The highest mountains in the world are in an area of atmospheric turbulence since it is here that masses of air from the steppes of central Asia and air from the low plains along the borders of the Indian Ocean meet. The winter months plunge the Himalayas into deepest winter. In summer a mass of air known as the monsoon drives moist sea air across the land. On meeting the high Himalayas, the moisture falls as fresh snow; between June and September conditions are terrible. Up until the end of April, the winter's snow still lies deep. Thus, all in all, the mountaineers have only six to eight weeks for their assault on the summit. And, even during these few clement weeks —the time before the monsoon— the area is often lashed by furious storms. Conditions are scarcely more propitious in the post-monsoon period. The tail-end of the monsoon is followed almost immediately by the first storms of autumn, so that there are sometimes no intervening spells of fine weather. For mountaineers aiming to achieve great heights in the Himalayas, it is not just a fight against the mountain and the altitude, but a fight against time.

The death-zone . . . the monsoon . . . having given an account of so many problems involved in climb-

Sherpas are accustomed from childhood to transporting heavy loads in difficult conditions.

Flatbread cooked over an open fire is regarded as a delicacy by the Sherpas.

Sherpa Tenzing during a visit to an alpine mountaineering school.

Sherpa Pasang at about 19,500 feet.

ing the Himalayas, it is time that something be said in their favour. For one there are the Sherpas, the faithful companions of all Himalayan mountaineers. They are a people who emigrated from the east and settled on the south side of the Himalayas (Shar—east: Pa—people). During the first expeditions to the Himalayas, they proved themselves to be outstanding bearers and mountaineers; today they are the mountain guides of the Himalayas. Their good humour, their wit and their optimism have restored the confidence of many an outsider. Their courage and faithfulness make them the best climbing companions. The most renowned of the Sherpas —such as Tenzing, who was on Mount Everest with Hillary, or Pasang who, with Tichy, climbed Cho Oyu—have since been round half the world, and have become famous figures, for whom television appearances mean no more than cutting a good step in the ice.

The Yeti story

The Sherpas are convinced that there is, in their homeland, a being which is half-man, half-beast and which lives high up on the moun-tain among the ice-clad cliffs. The Yeti!

To this day no foreigner has set eyes on this snowman. There are only the Sherpas' numerous accounts of its existence. It is said that a distant figure was seen heavily plodding its way across a glacier in a region where, for miles around, there could not possibly have been another human being on the move. It is occasionally claimed that the creature's roars have been heard. Other evidence consists of foot-prints in the snow and in soft soil, excrement, even a Yeti nest constructed from bushes that no man would have been able to tear out of the ground. The Sherpas say that it is probable that a foreigner will never see a Yeti because it is a very shy and cunning animal. It must be added, however, that no one has yet found a Yeti corpse or skeleton.

In 1960 an expedition, led by the conqueror of Everest, Sir Edmund Hillary, set out with the aim of "proving or disproving the existence of the Yeti". The expedition suc-ceeded in doing neither. No Yetis were sighted. The Yeti scalp kept in the Khumjung monastery was even flown to Europe to be scientifically examined—it proved to be that of a

The reputed scalp of a Yeti in the Khumjung monastery.

A Yeti is supposed to look something like this! The artist copied a photograph of what were said to be Yeti footprints. The photograph was taken at 17,810 feet by the Englishman Eric Shipton during the 1951 Everest Expedition. The footprints were over 11 inches long and could be followed for nearly 2 miles before they disappeared in rocky terrain.

The summit of Annapurna.

200–300-year-old bear. Nevertheless, no member of the expedition was later prepared to declare: "The Yeti does not exist."

Annapurna

As early as 1922, the British reached an altitude of 27,000 feet on Mount Everest. But setting altitude records is not the same thing as conquering summits. Fourteen mountains of over 26,000 feet are known in the Himalayas and, in the course of several decades, no expedition succeeded in reaching the summit of even one of them.

For this reason, the Himalayan researcher, Günther Oskar Dyhrenfurth, known as the "Pope of the Himalayas", placed the first ascent of a mountain over 26,000 feet on a par with the discovery of the North or South Pole. The first to be conquered was the 26,502-foot-high Annapurna I.

In fact the French expedition that achieved this feat originally planned to climb the 26,810-foot Dhaulagiri. It was the strongest team that France could produce at that time (1950). The leader was the energetic Maurice Herzog, and with him were such top-class mountaineers as Jean Couzy, Louis Lachenal, Lionel Terray, Gaston Rébuffat.

The expedition set out on 30th March but by the beginning of May they still had not found a possible approach route up Dhaulagiri. And in June the monsoon starts! At the eleventh hour the expedition switched from Dhaulagiri to Annapurna. The assault began in mid-May. Only three weeks were left available to the expedition.

On 3rd June 1950, at 6 a.m., Herzog and Lachenal leave Camp V, established at 24,050 feet. A terrible snowstorm has raged all night long. Not one of the mountaineers was able to get any sleep. At every fresh gust of wind they had held fast the tent-poles with their hands, and had made continual attempts to shake the newly fallen masses of snow from the roof of the tent. At daybreak the storm had relented. It is bitterly cold. Despite their specially insulated clothing, the climbers feel as though they are naked. Lachenal several times takes off his shoes and rubs his feet.

The two men continue to climb. To talk is too tiring. Gestures have to suffice. Yes, let us try that way. Suddenly a fierce wind beats at their faces. At their feet an awesomely long drop. They are standing on the summit of Annapurna. It is 2 p.m. For the first time ever, a 26,000-foot mountain has been climbed by man.

On 3rd June 1950 Radio Calcutta forecast 5th June as the start of the monsoon. Suddenly the sky clouds over. Nevertheless Herzog continues his celebrations. The experienced climber Lachenal is the first to recognize the danger and urges departure. There then begins a race against death.

Herzog, still flushed with victory, loses his glove on the descent. He does not think to put on his spare glove from his rucksack. Later his fingers have to be amputated. But he does not know that yet and when, in jubilant mood, he reaches Camp V, he shouts to Rébuffat and Terray,

"We have just come from the summit of Annapurna!"

We . . . But where is Lachenal? Where? Lachenal has fallen headlong on to a steep snowfield . . . he lies prostrate on the cold ice, staring into emptiness, minus his ice-pick, his snowcap, his gloves . . . he is rescued by Terray. 4th June 1950 . . . snowstorms on Annapurna. "That's the monsoon. If we stay here any longer we will all be dead", says one of the Sherpas in Camp II. The four men at Camp V descend to Camp IV but fail to find it and are forced to spend a terrible night in a crevice in the glacier.

5th June 1950 . . . Herzog and Lachenal have frostbite in the hands and feet. Rébuffat and Terray have become snowblind. They shout for help. No one hears them. They descend farther, are buried by an avalanche, free themselves and finally after a long struggle reach their comrades.

"We set off for Annapurna without a penny in our pockets and for us it has become a veritable goldmine which will enrich the rest of our lives", expedition leader Maurice Herzog said later, back at the Neuilly military hospital where they were trying to save the remnants of his frostbitten limbs.

The arrival at Paris airport of the seriously injured conqueror of Annapurna, Maurice Herzog. On the right of the picture is Gaston Rébuffat.

Death and triumph on Nanga Parbat

In 1953 Mount Everest became the second mountain of over 26,000 feet to be climbed, and in the same year Nanga Parbat (26,660 feet) became the third . . . at last! Fourteen European and seventeen local climbers had already died on Nanga Parbat. The first deaths . . . in 1895 the great English mountaineer A. F. Mummery and two native companions failed to return.

Overcoming an ice-fall with rope ladders on the Nanga Parbat expedition of 1934.

In 1934 a huge combined expedition of Austrians and Germans set off. Nine top-class mountaineers, 35 of the best Sherpas and 500 bearers. Right at the start of the expedition one of the leaders died of a lung inflammation. Large funeral, great mourning. Precious time passed. Then, at last the advance resumed. By early morning on 6th July, the leading group, the Austrians Peter Aschenbrenner and Erwin Schneider had already reached 25,500 feet. The two of them could easily have pressed on to the summit that very day but, on this expedition, as many mountaineers as possible were meant to, wanted to, reach the summit simultaneously. So Aschenbrenner and Schneider waited for their comrades to arrive. Then, together, they established a camp at about 24,400 feet. And that was a mistake, especially after the long delays at the base camp. On the mountainside a terrible price has to be paid for the slightest slip.

On the night of 6th July, the terrible monsoon snowstorms began. On 8th July it was decided to descend. Aschenbrenner and Schneider went on in front to test the three-foot-deep new snow, the three leaders and eleven Sherpas followed. The leaders—Wilo Welzenbach, Uli Wieland and Willi Merkl—together with six brave Sherpas—never returned; they lost their lives in the white hell of Nanga Parbat.

In 1937, a strong team of Germans was once more on its way up Nanga Parbat. On the night of 14th July seven leaders and nine Sherpas lay asleep in an encampment about 21,000 feet up . . . four days later the expedition doctor Uli Luft made his way up from the base camp, somewhat concerned that it had been so long since anything had been heard from the advance party. He made a terrible discovery—the 1937 German expedition to the Himalayas no longer existed.

Shortly after midnight on 15th July an avalanche of ice had buried all sixteen as they lay in their sleeping-bags. A recovery expedition was later only able to bring back the comforting news that the men had all died in their sleep—without having to endure the fears and struggles of a slow death. Three watches that were found on the dead all showed the same time of death.

1938 . . . yet another German expedition to Nanga Parbat. They found the corpses of Willi Merkl and his Sherpa Gyali—still well preserved after four years. Any further advances on the summit were prevented by snowstorms.

1939 . . . a small expedition sets out to reconnoitre a potentially better route up another flank of Nanga Parbat.

1939 . . . World War II starts. The expedition is interned. Heinrich Harrer and Peter Aufschnaiter escape from the internment camp to Tibet and arrive in Lhasa at the court of the Dalai Lama. Harrer's book *Seven Years in Tibet* later became a world best-seller. Harrer and Aufschnaiter, however, never could have reached such a prominent place in Lhasa if they had not had that quality that every good expeditionary must have—adaptability!

1950 . . . two Englishmen failed to return from Nanga Parbat. 1953 . . . a combined German and Austrian expedition to Nanga Parbat. The Tyrolean climber Hermann Buhl makes a lone and successful attempt on the summit. From the last camp to the top he covers a distance of four miles, climbing 4,000 feet in sixteen and a half hours, alone, without breathing apparatus,

feeling his way slowly, laboriously through fresh-fallen snow or up precipitous cliffs. Even tough, highly experienced Himalayan mountaineers would previously have found such a feat absolutely inconceivable at this altitude.

On the descent Hermann Buhl had to take a rest period, standing at an altitude of about 26,000 feet, on a cliff ladder that provided only enough room for his two feet. He had no sleeping-roll, no provisions, no drink. There were over 20 degrees of frost and he had forcibly to keep himself awake for, below him, the cliff dropped sheer away. To have fallen asleep—that would have meant certain death.

After Hermann Buhl had spent forty hours alone in the death-zone, he eventually arrived back at the camp where his friends Hans Ertl and Walter Frauenberger were waiting for him. At that time he was twenty-nine years old. A photograph, taken by Hans Ertl after his return, shows the face of a completely spent old man. Four years later, Hermann Buhl met his death on the Himalayan peak Chogolisa. A few years after the victory on Nanga Parbat, Walter Frauenberger also plunged to his death—he fell

Hermann Buhl. This picture was taken only a few days before his fatal fall on the 26,402-foot Chogolisa—only the second mountain of over 26,000 feet which he had tackled.

from an open window during a heart-attack. At the time it was suggested that his heart had been damaged during the Nanga Parbat ascent, and that, in the end, he too was yet another victim of the mountain.

Live and let die . . .

seems to be not only the motto of secret agent James Bond, but also of the highest Himalayan peaks. Yet it is probably beyond the comprehension of a non-mountaineer to see in a mountain something resembling a living being that has good moods and bad moods. From 1954 onwards, the 26,000-foot Himalayan peaks seemed to have only good moods.

The Italians climbed the 28,250-foot K2. According to the Pope of the Himalayas Dyhrenfurth, "a well-organized use of equipment, an outstanding team performance and, in addition, a final assault party ready to spare no effort in their attack on the summit. In consequence, even the mountain of all mountains was forced to bow to man's will."

In the same year a small Austrian expedition climbed the 26,867-foot Cho Oyu. Leader of the expedition: Herbert Tichy—world traveller, adventurer, researcher, philosopher, writer. It is paradoxical that the victor of Cho Oyu afterwards repeatedly claimed, "I am no mountaineer!" Indeed the Viennese Herbert Tichy has never been up the Hausberg near Vienna, a mountain of snow a mere 6,744 feet high!

1955 . . . it was the 27,790-foot-high Makalu that became the *montagne heureuse* (mountain of good fortune) of the French. For the first time every climbing member of an expedition reached a summit —over a period of three days. The

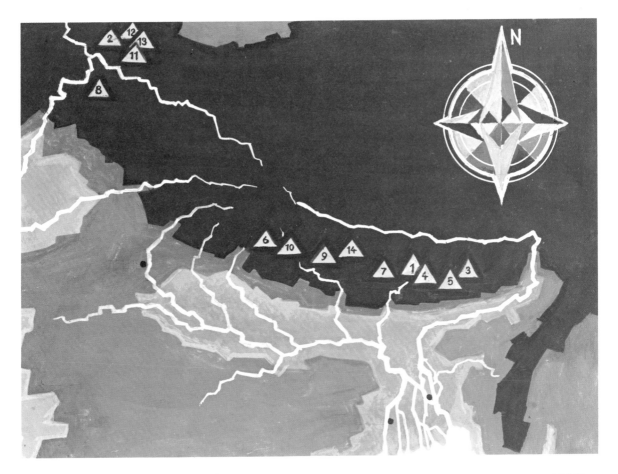

climbers arrived every day just before noon, when it was warm and there was no wind. The ascent of Makalu, which had been considered one of the most difficult mountains over 26,000 feet, was, in the view of the expedition leader, no more strenuous than an ascent of Mont Blanc.

1955 . . . the Britons George Band and Joe Brown conquered the 28,146-foot-high Kanchenjunga without actually setting foot on the summit, for Kanchenjunga is considered a holy mountain and permission for the ascent was only given on the condition that the highest point on the peak was not desecrated by the foot of man. The conscientious Britons kept to the agreement and refrained from treading on the last five feet of the summit. A curious episode in the annals of

HIMALAYAN PEAKS OVER 26,000 FEET	
Mount Everest	29,002
K2 (Mount Godwin Austen)	28,250
Kanchenjunga	28,146
Lhotse	27,890
Makalu	27,790
Cho Oyu	26,867
Dhaulagiri	26,810
Nanga Parbat	26,660
Manaslu (Kutang I)	26,658
Annapurna I	26,502
Gasherbrum I (Hidden Peak)	26,470
Broad Peak (Chogolisa)	26,402
Gasherbrum II	26,360
Shisha Pangma (Gosainthan)	26,290
Annapurna II	26,041

The world's 26,000-foot peaks.

Opposite: K2 (above) and Dhaulagiri, two 26,000-foot peaks. No photograph of a mountain of this size can give any true impression of its immensity.

Herbert Tichy and Sherpa Pasang at the summit of Cho Oyu.

In front of the radio transmitter at 21,124 feet on Dhaulagiri.

On expeditions, climbers often dig hollows in the ice to serve as camp stores and depots.

In the Himalayas there already stand many crosses . . .

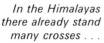

Himalayan climbing history. In 1956 Japanese mountaineers climbed Manaslu (26,658 feet), the Swiss scaled Lhotse (27,890 feet), the Austrians, Gasherbrum II (26,360 feet). In 1957 Austrian climbers conquered Chogolisa (26,402 feet) and in 1958 the Americans ascended Gasherbrum I (26,470 feet). A race between nations to the 26,000-foot summits. In 1960 a Swiss expedition made up also of Germans, Austrians and Poles reached the summit of the 26,810-foot Dhaulagiri. In 1964 the last of Earth's fifteen 26,000-foot mountains was vanquished by the Chinese: Shisha Pangma (26,290 feet).

Even nowadays the ascent of a 26,000-foot mountain is an adventure for which one can only prepare oneself well; even after the first lunar landing, six members of the advance party of a powerful Austrian expedition disappeared without trace on Dhaulagiri. The last radio message from 22,400 feet: "Tomorrow we will all be standing on the summit!" Then silence. In the days that followed, those in the base camp strained their ears to the

crackling radio. Occasionally they thought that they could detect the sound of faint voices, but every time it proved to be an illusion. Never again will a word be heard from the six men.

To this very day their deaths remain an unresolved mystery. We can only conjecture. An avalanche could not have buried them on their narrow ridge. Neither could the collapse of a single snow cornice have caused six experienced climbers to fall—for when on the move the spaces between each man was too great for that to happen. Only at one spot could the six have been standing close together—the summit. Did the summit's snow cornice break at the moment of greatest triumph? The mountain had won.

It is understandable then that climbers often regard a mountain almost as a living being, against whom they enter into battle.

CHAPTER 7

THE ULTIMATE IN CLIMBING

Turning points in the history of alpinism

The so-called Drei Zinnen in the Dolomites in fact consist of five peaks: Kleinste Zinne, Punta di Frieda, Kleine Zinne, Grosse Zinne, Westliche Zinne. Paul Grohmann considered his conquest of the summit of the highest pinnacle Grosse Zinne in 1869 as a victory over all three (or five) pinnacles. To attempt to climb one of the smaller pinnacles was a thought that never even crossed his mind. After all he had attained the highest point.

Ten years later mountaineers were already engaged in heated discussions as to whether the Kleine Zinne could be climbed. Michl Innerköfler, one of the best and bravest mountain guides of his time, took the view that: "Of course it's possible—if you've got wings!" Two years later he had not grown wings but, nevertheless, stood at the summit of the Kleine Zinne. People spoke of a turning point in the history of alpinism, because the ascent of an unimportant subsidiary peak was not classical mountaineering, but, in their opinion, nothing more than "senseless eccentricity".

In 1890 Lepp Innerköfler and Hans Helversen traversed the north face of the Kleine Zinne. Yet another turning point. The ascent of mountain walls and ridges had become as important to climbers as the conquest of summits once was. A member of the old school commented with bitter cynicism: "From now until the year 3000 the Alps will be no more than a climbing frame for glory-seekers, who want to be able to boast of a mountaineering 'first'."

Wrong! Even now, as this book goes to print, the Alps, where alpinism was born, have been so extensively climbed that there remains hardly a single "first" with which someone may achieve fame. The scene of great mountaineering feats has today moved to the mountains of the world. And even there, since the conquest of the highest and most prominent peak, mountaineering has reached a stage where the scaling of particular walls and ridges is rated an important goal in itself.

First ascents and first climbs

"Other men have conquered great islands with flat coasts; the island we have conquered is small, but is guarded by proud high cliffs." So wrote Otto Ampferer after his successful ascent of the 970-foot pinnacle Guglia di Brenta in 1899. Antoine de Ville on the Mons Inaccessibilis, Edward Whymper on the Matterhorn, Hermann Buhl on Nanga Parbat—they all experienced

On the north wall of the Westliche Zinne (west pinnacle).

The Drei Zinnen (three pinnacles). From left to right: Kleinste Zinne (smallest pinnacle), Punta di Frieda, Kleine Zinne (small pinnacle), Grosse Zinne (great pinnacle), Westliche Zinne (west pinnacle).

a particular kind of intoxication. The feeling that one is standing on a point where no man has ever set foot before. And a similar feeling is experienced by the first man to climb a wall or a ridge, when his fingers grasp a piece of rock never before touched by man.

In mountaineering there is, of course, a certain element of ambition and, in particular, that highly personal ambition to undertake something never before attempted.

Technique and equipment

Those scenes in films of mountains, that show a climber hanging by his fingertips from a narrow ledge are very impressive, but in reality a climber using only his hands would scarcely be able to climb a 300-foot cliff. Good mountaineers are rarely muscle men. The conqueror of Nanga Parbat, Hermann Buhl, was slender and had small biceps. All the same his leg muscles were as hard as iron. Emilio Comici, who climbed the most difficult rock faces in the world, had fingers as delicate as a pianist's. He was also a gifted guitar player. Maurice Herzog, the conqueror of Annapurna, could have been taken for a diplomat when dressed in his normal clothes. In fact he was a minister for a time. Neither the American John Harlin nor the Englishman Edward Whymper nor the outstanding Russian mountaineer Witalij Abalakow (as a child, a "weak, sickly little lad") were muscle men. It is not brute strength that counts in the moun-

the taut cable the Devil of the Dolomites worked his way across towards the stubborn needle of rock. He was running a huge risk. If the iron ball had jammed between unstable blocks. . . .

Even more fantastic was an

Above left: *Climbers in the northern limestone Alps.* Bottom left: *On the sandstone rocks of Saxon Switzerland.* Left: *On the Lofoten Islands.* Below: *On the granite peak of Mont Blanc. Wherever there are rocks, there are always mountaineering adventures to be experienced.*

tains, but skill in overcoming difficulties, in other words, alpine technique.

There were once mountaineers who carried throwing-anchors and used these to enable them to ascend smooth faces like sailors. In 1906 on the Guglia Edmondo de Amicis, the famous Dolomite guide Tito Piaz had to turn cowboy. After all attempts to climb the pinnacle had failed, Piaz (who, according to his fellow-countrymen, had sold his soul to the devil in order to be able to climb better) made a daring decision. He climbed the Punta Misurina, that lay opposite, and flung a cable, with an iron ball attached to the end, at the summit of the rock pinnacle, hoping that the iron ball would jam between two blocks of rock. Then, hanging from

attempt made in 1878 to climb the Dent du Géant (Giant's Tooth) in the Mont Blanc group. The mountaineers brought with them a cannon or, to be more precise, a rocket launcher! This was erected at the foot of the rock column, generally considered to be unclimbable. The intention was to fire a rocket with an extremely long cable over the Giant's Tooth, to secure the cable and then to make the ascent.

The plan, drawn up by English and Italian mountaineers, not only required considerable technical and financial resources but demanded, above all, a high degree of courage and skill, for it was with the actual ascent by the cable of the sheer wall of the Giant's Tooth that

The Giant's Tooth (13,055 feet).

Today an ascent of the Giant's Tooth is made a lot easier by the use of cables. The red standard rope ($\frac{7}{16}$ inch thick) gives some idea of the thickness of the cable.

A ring-hook in the rock. So that the climbing rope can run more smoothly two karabiners are suspended from it.

the adventure proper would begin.

Firing was begun. The first shot: the cable reached halfway up the wall. The second shot: the rocket struck the rock just below the summit. The third shot: the rocket and cable shot over the top of the summit and was flung back by the upcurrent of air from the other side. All further rockets were blown off course by the wind.

Many years later the Giant's Tooth was successfully climbed with the help of iron pegs, wooden wedges and many yards of cable.

In a roped party—which consists of two or three climbers linked together by rope—it is always the more accomplished and experienced man who leads the way. Should he have the misfortune to fall, it is the job of his partner to use the rope to break his fall (this always inflicts bad burns on the hands). The ropes generally used today are about 130 feet long and $\frac{1}{2}$ inch thick, and are made of a tough artificial fibre that eliminates the possibility of the rope breaking.

Before attempting particularly difficult pitches, pitons or pegs are driven into cracks in the rock, and the rope then attached by means of a karabiner (a ring that opens and shuts with a spring through which the rope is threaded). This is to minimize the distance the leading climber may fall. Pitons are also used to give extra support to the climber in positions where there is no handhold. On climbing routes that are used often these pitons are already in place.

Pitons and karabiners, which were originally intended for use only as safety devices, are today used as climbing aids on difficult routes. On overhangs or smooth rock faces, the climber uses them to support his rope ladder. And because there is too much friction exerted on a rope that has to run through twenty or more karabiners, on such climbs the mountaineer fastens himself to two ropes. If in a smooth rock face there are no cracks for pitons, then suitable holes are bored into the rock with a stone-drill. To overcome fissures, wood or plastic chocks can be used and these provide an equally good aid to climbing.

The surmounting of difficult sections of the cliff is generally extremely time-consuming. Sometimes a roped party only advances a rope's length in one day. Thus, for

Making sure you are well secured on a mountain is a form of life insurance. Whenever a climber climbs on ahead, his partner must be able to check his comrade's possible fall. So that he is not torn from the mountain wall by a violent pull on the rope, he must be well secured. Such security is made possible by pitons.

A piton is driven in . . .

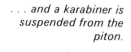

. . . and a karabiner is suspended from the piton.

Overhang at the so-called Death Chasm.

A difficult climb in Upper Schwabia.

The second climber follows on.

an extended stay on a cliff face, not only must food and water be carried but also bivouac equipment (sleeping-bags, hammocks, down-filled jackets, spare clothing). If a climb passes through mixed terrain, that is rock and ice (for instance, the north face of the Eiger), then, in addition to the rock-climbing equipment, a mountaineer has to carry ice-climbing gear—ice-pick or ice-axe, crampons, ice-pitons and ice-screws. A rucksack of such equipment sometimes weighs as much as 30 or 40 pounds.

If the summit is the target, then the trip to the summit is by no means the end of the undertaking. The descent often presents just as many difficulties, above all because it calls for considerably greater climbing skill than the ascent. Sheer cliffs that

This is how an overhanging rock is overcome—by using pitons and wire slings.

A climber on a difficult rock has a lot of material to carry—pitons of all sizes, karabiners, ropes, a hammer and a chisel.

can no longer be descended are overcome by abseiling. The climbing rope is wound round a projecting piece of rock or passed through a piton; then the mountaineer folds the rope across his shoulders and thigh (abseil position) and slides down. Having completed the manœuvre he regathers the rope by pulling on one end.

After a first ascent, the details of the route are recorded to assist all future climbers. For example: "Approach the rock face via the summit arête. Proceed up a distinctive chimney for 70 feet until an overhang is reached. Traverse 20 feet to the left, then up a steep cliff for 30 feet." Just as paths through the wilderness were once indicated by piles of stones placed at intervals along them, so the same technique is used. These marker posts are called cairns.

In addition to the route details, an assessment of the degree of difficulty is made according to a scale now accepted throughout the world. There are six degrees: I. easy; II. average; III. quite difficult; IV. difficult; V. very difficult; VI. extremely difficult. Pitches which can only be climbed by means of special aids (such as pitons) have their own scale of difficulty. AE 1 to AE 4 where A stands for artificial and E for expansion hooks.

Mountaineering is not learnt from the book but by experience. The beginner, starting on the first grade of difficulty, and even then only in the company of an experienced mountaineer, must spend many hours on the mountain, actively learning, until he is sufficiently advanced to attempt a climb of the fifth or sixth degree of difficulty.

The sixth degree

A modern nine-storey block of flats is approximately 100 feet high. The

A mountaineer in the abseil position. There are various methods of playing the rope over neck and thigh. This shows the so-called Vienna abseil position.

Opposite: *Overcoming a gigantic overhang in the Pyrenees.* Right: *Abseiling down a 260-foot tower of rock in the Wadi el Arnud (Valley of Pillars) in Israel.*

It is not the vigorous hand-over-hand climbing which is the most important, but the energy-saving technique.

north-west wall of the Civetta in the Dolomites is 3,700 feet high, in other words, thirty-seven times as high as a nine-storey block of flats. The Italians call it the Queen of all Walls.

In 1925, the Germans Emil Solleder and Gustav Lettenbauer climbed this enormous wall. The difficulties exceeded those of anything previously overcome in mountaineering. They start from the first moment of the climb and end approximately 100 feet below the summit. Furthermore, halfway up the wall there is a waterfall that has to be climbed through—ice-cold water in which every mountaineer expects to drown or to fall. The difficulties of the Civetta wall seemed at that time to represent the limits to which human endurance could be stretched; they could not be measured by any known scale of difficulty. When a new way of assessing difficulty was in fact devised, the Civetta wall came to be regarded as the first sixth-degree climb ever made.

The north wall of the Gross Zinne is only half as high as the Civetta wall. But, on the other hand, it is as smooth as the wall of a furnace. The first 650 feet have an overhang of fully 13 feet. It was this wall that forced Emil Solleder, the conqueror of the Civetta wall, to admit defeat, although he was convinced that, in a few years, it would be climbed by someone "madder than all the others".

The "madman" came in 1933. An increasingly large number of Italians had concentrated their full attentions on mountaineering with a passionate enthusiasm and had already accomplished several climbs of the sixth degree in the Dolomites. One of the best of them was Emilio Comici from Trieste. Comici came, and together with Giuseppe and

Angelo Dirnai, conquered the north wall after a struggle lasting three days. Their equipment consisted of 1,300 feet of cable, 490 feet of rope, 90 pitons and 50 karabiners. Soon after the ascent the first photographs made on the wall were released to the public. On seeing these pictures, even good mountaineers found it inconceivable that men could scale this sheer wall. Comici and his companions became celebrated as the miracle-workers of mountaineering, and their climb of the north wall as its supreme triumph.

Direttissima

Emilio Comici was also an aesthete. The ideal ascent of a wall should, in his opinion, proceed as straight as an arrow to the summit, should follow the line made by a drop of water falling from the summit into the depths . . . Direttissima! The word soon became a concept. However, even Comici considered a Direttissima on the north wall of the Grosse Zinne to be impossible.

In 1958, the north wall Direttissima was achieved. For five days, the

The north-west wall of the Civetta.

One of the
photographs taken on
the north wall of the
Grosse Zinne, the
ascent of which
caused such
excitement in 1933.

The climbers who
opened up the
Superdirettissima on
the north wall of the
Grosse Zinne in the
winter of 1963.

Lothar Brandler on
the north wall
Direttissima on the
Grosse Zinne.

Germans Lothar Brandler, Dieter Hasse, Jorg Lehne and Siegfried Low battled on the wall, often crossing smooth pitches only with the help of rock-screws. A daring route, but nevertheless not a real Direttissima, as was soon established after the climb, because the route diverged too much to the left of the path of a falling drop of water.

Thus, there was still a problem to be solved on the north wall of the Grosse Zinne. On 10th January 1963, in the midst of a bitterly cold winter, the Germans Rainer Kauschke, Peter Siegert and Gerd Uhner started off up the wall (in temperatures of 25 degrees below zero) in order—a mad idea!—to follow the line of a falling drop of water. The Germans did not want to wait until the next summer because they feared that others could beat them to the first real Direttissima ascent.

Snowstorms raged on the mountain. The three Germans inched their way farther and farther up, bivouacking in hammocks suspended from pitons, and hoisting their provisions up the rock on a 1,600-foot-long cable. They had ground staff. Every day one of their team mates made the journey from the Auronzo shelter to the foot of the wall to bring hot drinks and roast chicken, and to receive the climbers' orders for the next day.

Days passed. All three climbers now had frostbite and had to endure terrible suffering and spend half the night in massaging their limbs. On 22nd January the roped party had at last overcome the great overhang. In one day they had gained no more than 30 feet.

On 26th January, they reached the summit. They had spent seventeen days and sixteen nights on the wall. With the aid of 450 pitons the Superdirettissima had been achieved.

Expeditions on vertical climbs

After every attempt to climb the west wall of the Dru had failed, it was recognized as early as 1949 that this last remaining alpine problem was not to be overcome with traditional methods. Only expeditionary techniques could bring victory; instead of a roped party, a whole team was necessary to force its way by stages to the top. In 1952 the west wall of the Dru was conquered by the Frenchmen Lucien Berardini, Adrien Dagory, Marcel Laine and Guido Magnane in two drives in which a total of eight climbers participated. After the success of this first vertical expedition there was, once again, talk of a turning point in alpinism.

One thing is certain; after that time, mountaineers began to forge plans, the realization of which was to be reckoned in terms not of climbing hours and climbing days, but of climbing weeks. That also required a change in the mountaineers' mental attitudes. A walker who spends two weeks in the mountains making his way from summit to summit, continually derives fresh interest from the views of the surrounding countryside. The mind of a climber, suspended on a cliff face for two weeks, sometimes advancing only 30 feet in a day, can easily become deadened. And that is always dangerous on a mountain.

By 1961, the use of expedition techniques to climb perpendicular cliffs was so far developed, that four mountaineers—Walter Almberger, Toni Kinshöfer, Anderl Mannhardt and Toni Hiebeler—were able to realize a dream project that only ten or fifteen years earlier would have been described by even the most courageous alpinists as quite impossible and a suicidal undertaking; an ascent in winter of the north wall of the Eiger—the wall of death.

So far a total of almost fifty climbers have died on the 5,850-foot Eiger north wall, although, when approached along the route taken

On the Dru west wall.

In the so-called "suspended stance", the anchor man hangs in the ropes.

Above left: *Climbers on the rocks above the Danube Valley (at Wettenburg).*
Above right: *On the cliffs of the south coast of England.*
Bottom right: *In Saxon Switzerland.*
Bottom left: *Professional climbers —the so-called "rock clearers" of Salzburg, whose job it is to dislodge the disintegrating, precariously balanced rocks from the cliffs overhanging the houses.*

by the first climbers of 1938, it is by no means, as is often claimed, the most difficult wall in the Alps. The climbing difficulties presented by this route never exceed the fifth degree. However, what does make the Eiger wall one of the most dangerous in the world, is that it is of rock and ice. That means a hail of falling stones when the sun is shining, and avalanches after a change in the weather. And these changes occur often in the Bernese Oberland, which tower above the surrounding countryside, making the area a veritable cloud trap.

Imagine then, this in winter! There were many problems to be solved before the attack on the snow- and ice-covered wall. How was one to avoid frostbite? Hiebeler designed a new type of climbing shoe. Tablets to promote the circulation of the blood were a part of their supplies. What kind of nourishment could keep their bodies most active, whilst at the same time being easily digested by a stomach unsettled by the nervous tension? The nine days' supply of food that they took up the Eiger weighed $5\frac{1}{2}$ pounds per man. It consisted of malt extract, whole-wheat biscuit, Ovaltine, barley stew, tubes of condensed milk and jam, grape sugar, some ham and some dried meat.

Hiebeler, at that time thirty-one years old, was the brains of the expedition. The roped party was led by the twenty-seven-year-old Toni Kinshöfer, a man of great determination and much ability on both rock and ice who, a few years later, was to fall to his death while on a practice cliff.

On the ice-covered Hinterstoisser traverse the climbers encountered great difficulties. Hiebeler tells the story: "Suddenly, Almberger felt a violent jerk on the ropes leading to Kinshöfer and was almost dragged

off his feet. He reacted quickly and used all his weight to resist the pull of the rope. Anderl Mannhardt joined him, gripped the rope and helped him hang on. I, being some-what lower down, struck the ice-axe with my hammer, in order to drive it further into the snow. Seconds passed, without our hearing the slightest sound from Kinshöfer, who, judging by the pull on the rope, must have had a fall. The only thing we had heard had been the clatter of metal at the moment when Alm-

The Nordpfeiler on the Grande Jorasses climbed for the first time in 1938 by Riccardo Cassin and his companions, is characterized by a continuous succession of difficult climbing hazards.

The north wall of the Eiger—the ascent by Anderl Heckmair.

The north wall of the Eiger—the first winter ascent. Toni Kinshöfer on the Hinterstoisser traverse.

The north wall of the Eiger—the first ascent of the John Harlin-route. Dougal Haston on the first third of the ascent.

berger had been jerked forward. It must have been the pitons and karabiners that Kinshöfer was carrying. Apart from that and the rattling of a few splinters of ice, nothing.

"'Toni! . . .' I anxiously shouted—oppressive silence. . . .

"Then Almberger and Mannhardt shouted, then me again. 'It won't be that bad,' Mannhardt said. 'Toni always takes his time about answering; he has often driven me mad that way.'

"And indeed Kinshöfer at last replies: 'Nothing to worry about fellows. It was just a shelf of ice that's broken and thrown me about 15 feet. That's all—I am carrying on straightaway. Look, it's a bit easier going, now the ice-shelf's gone!'

"Thrown only 15 feet, that's all.

"That's Toni Kinshöfer all over; nothing can disturb his equanimity.

"What luck that two pitons were fixed in the rock. We were lucky."

Between 6th and 12th March 1961 the north wall of the Eiger was climbed for the first time in winter.

Six years later there was another sensation on the Eiger. Between 23rd February and 25th March, American, British and German climbers accomplished a Direttissima ascent of the north wall, with the aid of approximately 500 pitons and 30 screw-pitons, and 5,000 feet of rope.

The drive upwards was always made by a small group of climbers. With the help of climbing clamps the relief party would ascend the fixed ropes, whilst the other party would descend to the foot of the wall to recover. The fresh equipment and provisions would be ordered by radio ("Bring us some steaks as big as wash-bowls!") and brought up by a supply team also using the same fixed ropes to make the ascent.

On 22nd March, the American John Harlin, worked his way up the $\frac{1}{4}$-inch-thick nylon rope with his clamps, in order to join his comrades, who were already nearing the summit. On the next day—as he had said before starting out—the summit would be reached.

At 3.07 p.m. one of the observers, watching through binoculars, saw something dark fall down the wall on the Scheidegg, but thought at first that it was only a rucksack. It was not a rucksack, however. John Harlin had fallen! The fixed rope had snapped.

For John Harlin, art student, jet-pilot in the U.S. Air Force, and founder of the International School of Modern Mountaineering, the Direttissima ascent of the north wall of the Eiger had represented the greatest alpine problem still to be solved. His fellow climbers, who reached the summit a few days later, named the new route after him.

The John Harlin-route up the north wall of the Eiger certainly follows a straight line to the summit, but has the disadvantage that it is very liable to rock falls in summer. So, just a short time after it was accomplished, the problem of a summer Direttissima began to receive attention.

In 1969 this problem, too, was solved. Six Japanese climbers took thirty-two days and an enormous outlay of climbing materials to ascend the wall. At the head of the roped party there was often a woman, the twenty-seven-year-old doctor, Michiko Imai of Tokyo. After the climb, this elegant and attractive woman gave a lecture on *The Woman in The Mountains* at the annual international meeting of mountaineers in Trieste. She said

The ascent routes on the north wall of the Eiger. Unbroken line —route of the first ascent; dotted line —the John Harlin-route; broken line — the summer Direttissima of the Japanese.

that woman was only inferior to man in physical strength, but superior to him in strength of mind. In great undertakings on the mountainside, which require above all great strength of mind, a woman is, therefore, better equipped than a man. Up till now all great mountain problems have been solved by men, but the pioneering spirit is not lacking in women, as Valentina Tereshkova showed in 1963.

The Wall of Dawn

El Capitan—that is the name of the greatest free-standing monolith in the world. It is situated at the entrance to the Yosemite Valley in California. Its granite walls are 3,000 feet high and as smooth as polished marble—a challenge to American climbers. John Harlin was one of those who played an important role in the development of new aids for the ascent of such walls. Then within a few years even the very steepest of the walls of El Capitan had been conquered, only one remained—the Wall of Dawn.

The conquest of this wall by the forty-seven-year-old Warren Harding and the twenty-seven-year-old Dean Caldwell became a mountain adventure that the whole of America followed in the press and on television with the greatest of interest.

The two men started their climb on 23rd October 1970. For two years they had studied the wall in its every detail through binoculars, and photographed every stretch of the route with a special camera. Trials with new aluminium screw-pitons had shown that these facilitated a speedier advance up smooth parts of a wall. To bore the $\frac{3}{8}$-inch-deep holes required needed only seven minutes' work. Climbing equipment, hammocks and sleeping-bags, food (for twenty days) and drinking water (28 gallons) were carried in a bright red kit-bag that weighed 400 pounds.

The two climbers made only slow progress. By 27th October they had overcome just 750 feet of the wall. As they only had 600 feet of rope with them, it was impossible to withdraw down the sheer and, at times, overhanging face.

In the night of 3rd November a storm arose, that kept the two climbers in their hammocks for 107 hours. They were drenched to the skin and suffered—of their own free will—great hunger. They were saving their supply of food for the days when they would need all of their strength. On top of all this, Harding's hammock suddenly snapped and he was left hanging by one rope, in mid-air, 1,620 feet above the foot of the wall.

On 7th November the sun came out again. The climbers spent half a day drying out their clothing and their sleeping-bags. When Caldwell was at last able to continue climbing, a piton broke loose, and he fell the whole length of the rope to the bivouac. Distance achieved on that day: zero feet!

10th November . . . storms again . . . at first rain, then snow. 11th November . . . for days a great crowd of journalists, press photographers and cameramen had been gathered at the foot of the wall. A weather report forecast bad weather for the following days. It was, therefore, decided to start a rescue operation. Twenty-one rescuers, together with the necessary equipment, were landed on the summit plateau of El Capitan by helicopter. The two men on the wall were enraged, however, when they saw that they were to be rescued. "A rescue operation is not necessary, is not wished for, and will not be accepted", they scribbled on a piece of paper, that they threw down to people at the foot of the wall. They were only 1,000 feet from the summit.

On 15th November they consumed the last of their provisions . . . a can of sardines between two men. For the following days they had only a few vitamin tablets—and a tube of tooth-paste.

At midnight on 18th November, after twenty-seven days, Harding and Caldwell reached the summit of El Capitan, and were—as they put it —a little sad that this intrepid adventure had come to an end. They had been separated from all other men by only a few hundred feet, but what an infinite distance that represented.

The conquest of the Wall of Dawn gave final proof that, today, there is not a wall in the world that cannot be climbed by man.

CHAPTER 8

EXPEDITIONS

The Sourdough Expedition

Reaching, as it does, a height of 20,270 feet, Mount McKinley ranks as the highest mountain in North America. The gold prospectors of Alaska called it The Great, and truly this mountain is great. From the surrounding foothills, that reach a height of 1,300–1,600 feet above sea level, sheer cliffs and towering masses of ice and rock soar without interruption almost 20,000 feet to the snow-capped summit.

In 1906 Frederick Cook, a New York doctor, together with two companions made the journey to Mount McKinley. After unsuccessfully attempting to make the ascent, the party split up and Cook was left alone on the mountain with just one bearer. Then, on his return, he asserted that he had climbed the peak. He produced photographs he had taken on the summit, wrote a lengthy book on the subject, delivered innumerable lectures and was everywhere celebrated as the man who had conquered The Great —in reality it was all a fraud. Cook had never set foot on the summit of the mountain, the photographs had been taken from an innocuous peak in the foothills.

Soon after Cook's return there were many who doubted his story and, in order to confirm their suspicions, an expedition set off for Mount McKinley. This expedition was to go down in mountaineering history as the Sourdough Expedition. Sourdoughs was the name given in Alaska to the gold-miners of those times, because they always took yeast with them on their prospecting trips in order to be able to bake bread at all times.

Three sourdoughs set off to climb one of the toughest mountains in the world. From an innkeeper they borrowed 500 dollars—the expedition's only funds. Equipment— virtually non-existent. Clothing and provisions—inadequate for an undertaking of this sort. The sourdoughs had not even had the slightest experience of mountaineering. Doomed to die!

And yet—and this is the miraculous part of the story—they succeeded in setting up on the summit a 13-foot flagpole bearing the Stars and Stripes, and returning safely to the valley. Was it by good fortune or instinct that they found the only possible route to the summit area. Untiringly the three gold-prospectors worked their way up the steep Muldrow glacier, bypassing mighty towers of ice, leaping across deep crevasses, pitching their tent on the ice evening after evening. They were lucky with the weather and with their climbing. The three sourdoughs had made only one mistake in their venture and it robbed them

A descent from the summit of Mount McKinley in 42 degrees of frost.

The base camp of a small expedition, and above it the summit of Mount McKinley.

This photograph, published in 1907, is a curiosity. It purports to show Frederick A. Cook on the summit of Mount McKinley —on which he never in fact set foot.

of total victory—they had completely disregarded the topography of the great mountain.

In fact, Mount McKinley has two summits. The south summit is the higher—in other words the real summit. The north summit is approximately 350 feet lower. At high altitudes it is, however, very difficult to judge the relative heights of distant peaks with the naked eye. When the sourdoughs came to make their choice from the two summits, they chose the wrong one!

Four years later, Archdeacon Hudson Stuck stood, with his four companions, on the true summit. The wind had long since torn the sourdoughs' flag to tatters; only the flagpole, tall and stark against the sky, still remained. Archdeacon Stuck and his companions placed a small cross of birchwood on the south summit of Mount McKinley. Then they sang a *Te Deum*.

No mountaineer takes birchwood with him today to make a cross. On the other hand, he is required to carry a radio, if he applies at least a year in advance to the Mount McKinley National Park Authority

People are forbidden to take skis on to Mount McKinley, as it is too dangerous. Mountaineers use Eskimo snow-shoes.

These mountaineers on the summit of Mount McKinley look like strange monsters in their modern clothing, which gives them special protection against the cold.

95

View from the
Ruwenzori.
Opposite: *The summit
of the Ruwenzori.*

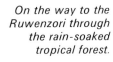

On the way to the
Ruwenzori through
the rain-soaked
tropical forest.

for permission to climb North America's highest peak. He must also be able to produce a declaration of support from a mountain rescue group. The sudden deteriorations in the weather are still feared.

Ruwenzori—the rain-maker

The Sourdough Expedition of 1910 was undertaken by three men. What a contrast to the 1906 Ruwenzori Expedition, which consisted of more than 400!

The story to date: two German missionaries in 1848 were the first Europeans "to look upon the wonders of Africa in person—snow-capped mountains which scorn the Equator". The then famous London geographer, Cooley, did not believe in these mountains on the Equator.

A short rest for the
porters on the long
march to the
Ruwenzori.

The missionaries must have experienced an optical illusion, their account has a dream-like quality. "I'd rather attribute such anomalies to the traveller than to Nature", Cooley wrote. Neither did the famous geographer believe the writers of antiquity, who reported that the Nile had its source in the mountains. The astronomer and geographer Ptolemy, who lived about A.D. 150 in Alexandria, named these the Mountains of the Moon.

In 1888 the African explorer, Henry Stanley, became the first white man to reach the foothills of the Mountains of the Moon. In this region there are only about a dozen days in the year when it does not rain. Thus Stanley called the 16,637-foot-high mountain of the land Ruwenzori, which in the local dialect means "rain-maker". In 1906, the Duke of the Abruzzi set out to climb Ruwenzori.

Africa's highest mountain, Kilimanjaro (19,159 feet) had already been climbed in 1889. Ten years later the second highest mountain in Africa, Mount Kenya (16,900 feet) had been overcome, yet the "rain-maker" had resisted all attempts to climb it.

Prince Luigi Amedeo of Savoy, Duke of the Abruzzi, member of the Italian royal household and

Admiral of the Fleet (1873–1944) was not only one of the best mountaineers of his time but also the perfect manager of an expedition. The members of his expedition were not only specially selected mountaineers, but also highly gifted doctors, geologists and botanists. In addition, there was a writer to make the reports of the expedition, and Vittorio Sella, the best mountain photographer of his time. To carry the supplies for the expedition, which was equipped to sustain a siege of many weeks, almost 200 bearers were engaged. Further, as a protection against the hostile tribes of the region, a strong contingent of

askari provided an escort. When moving in single file, the expedition resembled a giant snake winding its way through the soaking undergrowth. This column of men extended over five miles.

Rain, mists, swamps . . . moisture that permeated cloth and leather . . . fog that obscured all visibility and killed all spirit. . . .

The giant snake crept on. At last the mountain was reached. Then, the long wait in rain-drenched tents until a period of good weather. But is there ever good weather on Ruwenzori? There is indeed, one must just have patience and enough supplies for a long wait. The Duke

Mount Kenya and Kilimanjaro, the highest mountains in Africa.

The ice-field on Mount Kenya has yet to be traversed. The photograph opposite was taken during a fruitless attempt in 1968. The mountaineer would climb at dead of night so as not to encounter ice softened by the heat of the sun.

The target of
mountaineers in the
Antarctic: the
12,334-foot Mount
Erebus.

The 2½-mile-wide
glacial front of the
Tempelfjord on
Spitzbergen.

of the Abruzzi had both. For that reason, he and three guides triumphed.

The only way he could tell he was standing on the summit was that the ground no longer went up. For, in the course of the climb, the weather had deteriorated again. The conqueror of the "rain-maker" could not even see the faces of his companions if they stood more than three yards away from him!

The leaders and members of expeditions

The Duke of the Abruzzi's task in organizing and leading an expedition was eased by his great wealth and inherited authority. Yet, every expedition leader has been of the opinion that the preparations for an expedition use up as much nervous energy as the actual ascent itself.

Once the target of an expedition has been determined, and the members chosen, the next job—it may sound strange—is the paperwork. Entry permits, travel permits, climbing permits and visas have to be obtained. Correspondence with the participants on the expedition, correspondence concerning the provision of finances and equipment. Letters, telegrams, telephone calls and cables. At last the day of departure arrives.

From now on the expedition leader must, above all, be a good

psychologist. Mountaineers are individualists, and to lead a whole group of them is not an easy job. After many weeks of being together, everyone becomes more conscious of everyone else's strengths and particularly of their weaknesses. Then there is the physical and mental load. Once, in an advance camp, two mountaineers started to fight each other so fiercely that the tent collapsed. Origin of the dispute: it had got on the one mountaineer's nerves that, for the last three days, the other had talked almost non-stop about his stamp collection.

There is a fundamental principle underlying expeditions: only the best of the best have all the odds on their side! Only those who at the decisive hour on the mountain are the best, have everything on their side. A famous name or famous past deeds do not count on an expedition. Only the present matters!

1954 . . . the Italians on K2.

Achille Compagnoni and Lino Lacedelli reached their last camp before the summit, at a height of 26,160 feet. They still had to overcome another 2,000 feet and they badly needed oxygen. Walter Bonatti, whose fitness would have been sufficient for the attempt on the summit, took on the job of carrying the heavy oxygen cylinders up the mountain (with the bearer Mahdi).

Mountaineering goals in the desert. Basalt towers of the Hoggar range, some of which reach a height of almost 9,750 feet.

Climbing on the Hoggar.

Petit Dru (11,133 feet) with the Bonatti Pillar on the right beneath the summit.

Later the two of them had to bivouac on a tiny area of ground that they had cleared with their ice-axes, situated almost 26,000 feet up on a steep ice-slope. It was a terrible night.

Compagnoni and Lacedelli reached the summit. And Bonatti? He wrote later: "I sometimes burst into tears at remarks about K2. No one can imagine just how much it makes me suffer!"

Bonatti found a medicine to cure his inner suffering. An unusual medicine, to say the least. He prescribed for himself a solo climb on the south-west pillar of the Dru—a vertical pillar of rock with overhangs like an inverted stairway.

On 17th August 1955 Bonatti set off up the pillar. His **only** companion was a 66-pound rucksack containing pitons, provisions, etc. The night before he had felt like a man condemned to death.

On the fourth day Bonatti was already bivouacking in the middle of the Red Plates, the most problematic zone of the pillar. His hands were wounded and swollen, every contact with the rock caused unbearable pain.

On the fifth day the lonely climber reached a point where he could go neither forward nor back. Bonatti felt his end had come: "Physically and mentally exhausted, I stayed motionless for a whole hour, unable to think, attached to this one piton, which supported us, the rucksack and me, in oppressive solitude." Bonatti refers to "us" when he is talking of himself and his rucksack! In fact, on this solo climb, he often talked to his rucksack as if it were a living being.

Bonatti escaped from the corner he was in by daringly swinging across the rock face on his rope. When, six days later, he reached the summit, he had the feeling that he had achieved happiness enough to last him for the rest of his life.

K2 and its consequences! Bonatti had amassed such a store of energy for the conquest that only the ascent of another summit could release him from its power. For a year Bonatti suffered under this load until, with the conquest of the south peak of the Dru he was finally able to free himself from it. No one, not even an expert, can make even an approximate estimate of the limits to which a brave man can stretch human endurance and will power, on the mountains.

1970 . . . another German expedition on Nanga Parbat. Aim of the expedition: the conquest of the 14,600-foot-high Rupal face, the highest wall of rock in the world.

The brothers Gunther and Reinhold Messner were the first men ever to reach the summit of Nanga Parbat via the difficult and dangerous Rupal face—and this without breathing equipment. There they got altitude sickness. A descent back down the ascent route was considered by Reinhold Messner to be too risky, and to have waited for help from the other climbers was, at this height—the death-zone—out of the question. Yet it was imperative that Gunther Messner reach the safety of the lower regions as quickly as possible. Reinhold decided to make the descent on the other side of the mountain, down the 13,000-foot Diamir face.

Let us be clear just what this decision meant. On the Diamir face there were no advance camps and no base camp. Just 13,000 feet of snow, ice and rock, and, at the foot of the wall long glaciers followed by vast

tracts of impenetrable wilderness. No human beings from the summit to . . . who knows where? And in addition the Diamir face itself is no easy climb. After the first successful ascent in 1961 one of the climbers had died of exhaustion during the descent. He was Sigi Low, one of Germany's best mountaineers.

The brothers started the descent in what was for them unknown territory. The lower they came, the more Gunther recovered. Bivouac. The mountaineers had only thin nylon blankets as a protection against the bitter cold. Up at first light. They soon reached the lowest section of the face, where the threat of avalanches was at its greatest, and now they had to endeavour to cross the steep slopes, before the snow face was exposed to the full intensity of the sun's rays.

Now there was no problem. Each brother made his own way forward.

Nanga Parbat—the Rupal flank from the south-west.

Reinhold Messner.

The Andes.

Reinhold finally reached a safe position and waited there for Gunther. But Gunther did not arrive. Reinhold shouted. No answer. Reinhold retraced his steps and saw the huge blocks of a recently fallen avalanche. His brother had been buried beneath them. Once again Reinhold made camp. Then, with freezing limbs he staggered on through the wilderness back towards his fellow men.

The most daunting mountains in the world

The longest mountain chain in the world is the 5,000-mile Andes in South America. At their southern end, in Patagonia, there are mountains that are probably the most daunting in the world. There are bizarre granite bosses that rise over 10,000 feet, and which even on the easiest slopes provide climbs of the sixth degree of difficulty. But that is not all. What is really terrifying on these mountains is the frequency of rapid drops in temperature which leave the rock covered with a thick sheet of ice. When, on those rare days of fine weather, the temperature rises again this ice breaks up causing an uninterrupted hail of ice and rock. And then, on top of all this, there are the fierce storms that rage around these mountains.

In 1952 the Frenchmen Guido Magnane and Lionel Terray ascended the 11,173-foot-high Cerro Fitz Roy, "the most challenging mountain in the world", as they at that time rightly claimed. On a previous attempt they had been forced to return by one of the dreadful storms. They had found, to their amazement, that the abseil ropes they had tried to lower, were held suspended like flapping flagstays by the force of the wind. Only when they tied stones to their ropes were they able to descend. Such was the force of the storm. Nevertheless Cerro Fitz Roy was conquered.

Of the neighbouring Cerro Torre (10,166 feet) it was claimed: "There is not the remotest chance of climbing this peak. Any hope to the contrary is almost too ridiculous for words." In 1959 Cerro Torre was climbed by the Italian Cesare Maestri and the Austrian Toni Egger. Maestri afterwards recounted an experience that gives a most vivid impression of what the storms in this region are really like. Together with a few companions he had reached the foot of the ice-covered boss. Then suddenly there was a muffled crack. Maestri watched a snow cornice break away from the summit. A cloud of ice and snow plunged down the rock face towards the very spot where Maestri and his friends were standing.

But it was precisely the force of the storms in these mountains that saved them! Maestri's account is staggering. "Almost miraculously the falling snow cornice hangs suspended halfway down the rock face. Then, after a few tremors, it is gradually, forced back along the wall, as if lifted by some unseen power. It is a vision reminiscent of the apocalypse. This vast mass of ice and snow, as big as a house, that had fallen half the length of the rock face with devastating speed, is slowly lifted back along the same route by the sheer violence of a powerful current of air. Slowly, like a stage curtain, the cornice rises, hovers over the summit of Torre and disappears from view before even the smallest piece of it has fallen on us."

Despite storms, ice and glaciers, Cesare Maestri and Toni Egger then went on to reach the summit of Cerro Torre. They lodged their axes in the ice, and clinging to them for support against the raging storm,

Cerro Fitz Roy.

knelt and embraced each other . . . "it is not a joyful embrace, because fear grips our hearts. An evil wind is bringing warmer air from the west. Soon the snow will start to melt slightly and begin to slip away in innumerable avalanches."

The howling of the storm and the thunder of the avalanches drowned any conversation between the two mountaineers as they abseiled down the cliffs. One bivouac and then another on the descent. It was now their sixth day in the steep cliffs of Cerro Torre. In order to keep out of the paths of avalanches, they lowered themselves on ropes down cliffs as smooth as glass. In order to facilitate their abseiling they had to drive ice-pitons into the rock. To fix one piton takes a thousand blows of a hammer and pitons are always fixed in pairs for safety's sake.

Toni Egger did not return from Cerro Torre. While he was abseiling, an avalanche of ice once again thundered down the cliffs. Stunned by the air pressure and the falling masses of snow, Maestri clung fast to the safety rope that linked him to Egger. And then, when the avalanche had passed, Maestri pulled on the

One of the shelters on Aconcagua. This one is at about 13.000 feet.

rope. He was able to take it in without effort. There was no one hanging from it. The avalanche had broken through the rope and torn Toni Egger down with it. Within the space of a minute, Cesare Maestri had become the loneliest man on earth.

Reinhold and Gunther Messner on Nanga Parbat . . . Cesare Maestri and Toni Egger on Cerro Torre. In each case only one man returned alive. The luckier man.

Fashionable Aconcagua

On some maps Aconcagua is still marked as being over 22,750 feet although, according to the latest surveys, it is supposed to be only 22,597 feet. It remains, however, the mightiest mountain of South America.

As early as 1883, the German Paul Güssfeldt reached a height of more than 22,125 feet on its slopes. Then he gave up. Not because of the technical difficulties, but because of the endless fields of debris where for every step up, the foot slips back half a step down the dry scree slopes. And, in those altitudes, swept by literally breathtaking winds, that is much more exhausting than climbing a difficult rock face.

Towards the end of 1896, an English expedition came to conquer the "greatest heap of debris in the world"—as Aconcagua was called. The account of the climb is not a story of intrepid mountaineering. It is more like a collection of hospital medical histories—mountain sickness, altitude cough, agonizing headaches, heartburn and aching lungs, chilblains and flu, stomach cramp and breathing difficulties. Assault after assault stretched human endurance to the limit.

The leader of the expedition, Edward A. Fitzgerald, collapsed (on 14th January 1897) 1,000 feet below the summit, after he had had a trifle to eat during a rest period.

The Swiss mountain guide, Matthias Zurbriggen, carried on alone on the same day and, finally, with his last reserves of energy, reached the summit. He had stretched his body to its limits in order to gain the victory so desperately sought after by the expedition. However, the other members of the expedition also wanted to set foot on the summit. A further attempt was thwarted by a snowstorm.

Then, in February 1897, Aconcagua was finally climbed again, this time by the Englishman Stuart Viner and the Italian guide Nicola Lanti. But the expedition leader, Fitzgerald, the initiator and organizer, the very soul of the whole enterprise and one of the best mountaineers of his time, was once more driven back by altitude sickness.

Today, Aconcagua has become a fashionable mountain. Since 1951 there has stood, at a height of about

Opposite: This is what Aconcagua looks like to a passenger on the Trans-Andean Railway, which climbs to a height of 10,400 feet.

A gigantic avalanche thunders down the 9,750-foot south wall of Aconcagua.

21,000 feet, perhaps the highest-placed mountain hut in the world—the Juan Peron refuge. There is even a mule track leading up to a height of 21,900 feet. Today many climbers ride up to this point. Even so—according to the account of one of the leading experts on the mountain—only one in ten has enough strength left to climb the last 650

The mighty massif of Mount Logan.

Norman H. Read, wanted to find out whether the passing years had aged him at all. He wanted to try once more to climb Mount Logan, which no man had set foot on since. Twenty-five years is a long time. Read wanted to use the advances of modern technology so he had himself flown (together with his companions) to a position fairly high up

feet to the summit on his own two legs. Clearly the human organism requires a gradual acclimatization.

Flying mountaineers

It was not until 1925 that the second highest mountain of North America (after Mount McKinley) was conquered: the 19,850-foot-high Mount Logan in Canada. For months the climbers battled against ice, storms, freezing conditions (34 degrees below zero) until, finally, after a sudden drop in temperature—it became a race against death.

Twenty-five years later, one of the members of this expedition,

Mount Logan. And there the weather deteriorated.

The mountaineers had to wait eighteen long days suffering from cold and hunger, until finally the plane arrived with their provisions and equipment. Of course the plane was unable to land in the drifts of newly fallen snow. The gear had to be dropped, and was scattered over an area of eight miles. Some of it could not be recovered. With the barest of rations, the expedition had to set off on the second ascent of Mount Logan. Read, in doing this, was relying on a food cache that had been left at a height of 18,330 feet in 1925. The assault party did not, in fact, find this food cache, and had to go without. Nevertheless they managed to reach the summit.

It was the aeroplane, not man, that had failed on this expedition. In 1960, on the ascent of Dhaulagiri in the Himalayas (a peak over 26,000 feet), it was again the plane that failed. A specially equipped plane was supposed to carry the

Mountaineers indignantly reject such a way of reaching summits. Why? Because that would go against the whole spirit of mountaineering. The mountain is to be climbed by man's effort alone. Even so, were alpinism to have had its beginning today, in such a technologically advanced age, the rules of the alpine sport would have developed very

The transport plane of the Swiss Dhaulagiri Expedition before the landing at 16,250 feet.

expedition's supplies to a height of 18,500 feet. This was only partly successful. Finally, dogged by engine trouble and forced landings the plane was grounded as being beyond repair. Man, however, still conquered Dhaulagiri.

Of course it would be possible today to land men on the highest peaks of the world from specially designed planes. Such an "ascent" would depend only on the technical skill of the pilot. It would even be possible to put a seventy-year-old man (provided he had breathing apparatus) on the summit of Mount Everest, even a man who had never before set foot on a mountain.

differently. It is likely that, if none of the great mountains had been conquered before 1980, then the first to reach the summits would probably have flown not climbed there.

To this day, the aeroplane has not proved particularly useful in the high mountain ranges. Even when expedition members have been flown to base camps situated high up the mountain, it has been of little advantage. The time saved has to be spent in acclimatization. For example, some members of the Swiss expedition to Dhaulagiri became extremely mountain sick and had to be flown back again from the

acclimatization camp situated at 16,400 feet.

Better equipment . . . better men?

The mountain range to the northwest of the Himalayas, not far from the border between Russia and China, is called Pamir or the Roof of the World.

The 26,163-foot Pik Kaufmann, later called Pik Lenin, was first climbed by the Germans Eugen Allwein and Karl Wien and the Tyrolean Erwin Schneider in 1928. On this climb, they allegedly managed to ascend to a height of 4,300 feet and to descend again, all in one day. The Russians later had their doubts about the authenticity of this claim. For, in 1934 a Russian expedition, which succeeded in reaching the summit only after days of struggle (and carrying a bust of Lenin in a rucksack), found no cairn nor any other sign of man's presence there. Furthermore, people did not believe it possible for men to go up and down 4,300 feet in one day.

The summit of Pik Lenin, with the plaster bust of Lenin and the decorative flags marking the International Alpine Congress.

Camp beneath the summit of Pik Lenin.

Erwin Schneider comments: "We built no cairns. We were simply glad to begin the descent at once; the cold was so bitter." The temperature was more than 30 degrees below zero. All three alpinists returned with frostbitten feet. Erwin Schneider continues: "If the Russians don't believe us, that's their affair. I find it undignified for mountaineers even to discuss such things amongst themselves."

The Russians' doubts stemmed from the fact that, at that time, their top mountaineers took substantially longer to make progress on Pik Lenin than the Germans had. Only now, in the last few years, when the Russian alpinists have learnt to make speedy progress and are able to accomplish the same feats as Schneider and his party, have they withdrawn all their accusations and recognized the summit climb made by the Germans. Indeed, they have rectified their mistake by subsequently awarding a gold medal.

While it is possible in most sports to observe a continuing rise in performance, in alpinism there were achievements of the highest order which took place many decades ago and which to this day remain unsurpassed. This is recognized without jealousy by the best mountaineers of our day. Above all, they are impressed by the primitive equipment and (by today's standards) the

Kirgisenjurten at the foot of the Roof of the World.

111

inadequate provisions, with which these feats were accomplished by the men of the time.

The Playground of the World

Round about the middle of the last century, the Englishman, Leslie Stephen, called the Alps the Playground of Europe. Nowadays, mountains wherever they stand—whether it be in the sandy deserts of Africa or the icy wastes of the Arctic and Antarctic—have become the Playground of the World.

The aeroplane has made our world smaller and on every mountain are climbers searching for one of the last real adventures of our time. They are making first ascents, they are climbing every mountain which has something to be ascended or scaled for the first time. In 1968, when the Route Caesar Augustus in the steep rocks of Capri was traversed for the first time, the last peg was driven into the retaining wall of the Hotel Caesar Augustus. On the occasion of the first ascent of a rock face in the Sahara the key to the climb presented itself in the form of a mighty overhanging thorn bush. The climbers conquered this key position by setting fire to the thorn bush and reducing it to ashes. And, in the Himalayas, where there are high passes of almost 18,000 feet, there was the case of climbers who climbed down from such a pass in order to be the first conquerors of a 15,000-foot peak.

The age of the large expeditions is certainly coming to a close. Where, formerly, the conquest of a 26,000-footer was almost always a national occasion, nowadays the first ascent of the flank of a 26,000-footer, in itself an equally impressive achievement, scarcely arouses any special interest amongst the general public. But it has been the widespread interest, recently often nurtured by the press and broadcasters, which up to now has guaranteed the material requisites for all the large expeditions.

The future belongs to the inexpensive small expeditions . . . a few companions who set off with equipment which they have saved up to buy.

"Penitent snow" is the name given to melting ice in tropical and sub-tropical highland regions. According to an old legend, the bizarre shapes are sinners who have been turned into ice.

CHAPTER 9

NORDIC VERSUS ALPINE

Across Greenland on skis

In the autumn of 1888 the Norwegian, Fridtjof Nansen crossed Greenland from east to west with some companions. Why? "You could give a long answer to that", wrote Nansen. "One could draw attention to the effect such a highland of ice and snow must have on the climate of all those parts of the earth which border on it, showing how every single part of the earth's surface is directly connected to all the others; however, just the fact, that Greenland's interior makes up a portion of the surface of this planet and, indeed, a not wholly unimportant portion, is sufficient to awaken a desire to get to know it and not to rest until that has been achieved, even if the path to it costs some people their lives."

Nansen and his companions pulled their sledges of equipment on skis for forty days and over 350 miles, through the interior of Greenland. On the journey a summit of 8,700 feet had to be conquered. One of Nansen's companions sighed: "Almighty God, can men have such little regard for themselves, that they can let themselves in for something like this!" That is what Fridtjof Nansen relates in his book *Across Greenland on Skis*. This book, originally published in 1891, had an effect which the author himself had not predicted. It made its readers less enthusiastic about adventures in cold Greenland but, at the same time, it increased their interest in trying out such skis for themselves.

The ski duel

The skis, on which Nansen and his companions made their way through Greenland, were heavy oak boards with leather straps, 8 feet 6 inches in length. When you wanted to start off you simply got yourself moving somehow and, if you started to move too quickly, you threw yourself sideways into the snow, or you slipped quickly out of the straps and used your shoes as a brake! With such fastenings, changing direction was always a work of art. In spite of this, the first peak of over 9,000 feet to be ascended in the Alps, the 10,000-foot Sonnblick, was ascended using these skis and, from there, the journey to the Kolm-Saigurn, which lay 5,300 feet farther down was made in thirty-two minutes. And, that same year, the English writer, Conan Doyle, the creator of Sherlock Holmes, began an extended alpine skiing tour, from Davos over the mountains to Arosa.

Matthias Zdarsky from Lilienfeld in Lower Austria was the man who later created the correct basic technique for skiing on mountains, both

The Eiger with its north wall. On the right of the picture is the white flank down which Sylvain Saudan skied.

through his book *Alpine Skiing Technique*, published in 1896, and by the ski-fastening which he invented. At first, however, Zdarsky was harshly criticized by the supporters of the Norwegian skiing style. In his fastening, the shoe was fixed to the ski and, it was claimed, could result in terrible bone breakages. They did not think much of Zdarsky's skiing technique which only used one stick. Zdarsky had a fiery temperament and was a man who ardently defended his own ski-fastening and skiing style. However, his opponents only saw him as a dreamer. And so the famous "ski war" between the supporters of the Norwegian technique and those of the Lilienfeld technique began.

Nansen plunges into a glacial crevasse. An illustration from the famous book Across Greenland on Skis.

An instructional photograph from Zdarsky's textbook Alpine Skiing Technique.

Zdarsky finally found a great ally in the well known mountain climber Willi Rickmer Rickmers. The latter donated a prize of 3,000 crowns, to be awarded to the man who could beat Matthias Zdarsky at skiing. At that time 3,000 crowns was a considerable sum. In 1906, the famous Norwegian skier Hassa Horn presented himself as a challenger. The duel was to be held on the steep Breiten Ries which lies on the snow-capped mountains near Vienna.

The Norwegian, however, did not stand a chance. According to the skiing historian, Erwin Mehl, Matthias Zdarsky was the best skier of his time. By the year 1896 he had already skied at over 62 miles an hour over a distance of 270 yards on a slope with a gradient of 1 in 5, he could do the Auerbach somersault on skis (that is a backwards somersault, while descending), and executed a jump of more than 65 feet from a tower which he had built himself.

The duel did not take place. Hassa Horn saw Zdarsky ski, realized that he was the better man—and withdrew. The Lilienfeld technique had won; the ski war was at an end. The same year Zdarsky made skiing history once again; he laid out the first slalom course on the Muckenkogel near Lilienfeld ($1\frac{1}{4}$ miles in length, a drop of 550 yards through 85 gates).

Skiing—an extreme

Skiing continued to develop. At first skis were seen only as the means to an end. They were to enable men to push forward into the snow-covered mountains. By 1911 Mount Fujiyama had been conquered using skis and Mount Kilimanjaro was next in 1912. Later people began to concentrate increasingly on beautiful ski descents. Nowadays it is all the rage to go skiing along small cross-country tracks and, once again, it is a lone wolf who has been causing a stir in the last few years. Like Nansen and Zdarsky this man is receiving more attention than all the racing skiers engaged in trying to knock tenths of a second off their records. He is Sylvain Saudan, born in 1936 in Valais.

In 1967 a report appeared in the alpine newspapers stating that the first-ever descent on skis of the Spencer Couloir had been made on 23rd September. The Spencer

Reproduction of a 4,000-year-old rock painting from Norway, showing a hunter on skis with a throwing stick and a mask in the shape of a hare's head.

The Marinelli Couloir on the east wall of Monte Rosa which was descended on skis by Sylvain Saudan.

The Spencer Couloir on the Aiguille de Blaitière.

Couloir is a slope on the Aiguille de Blaitière in the Mont Blanc group. This report seemed incredible to everyone in the Alps. To conquer this steep ice-channel you would normally need someone skilled in the use of climbing irons, or hard work with a pick; and this same ice-channel had been conquered on skis?

In the following year the same "madman" descended the Whymper Couloir on the Aiguille Verte, which has gradients of up to 11 in 20. He added to that the daunting Gervasutti Couloir on Mont Blanc du Tacul, once again in the autumn: its height is 2,640 feet with a gradient of 11 in 20, in some places even more than that. But, the most important thing about it was that there was such a great risk of avalanches of ice or rocks. Who was this madman?

To be sure, people had already made ski descents between the white walls of precipices before this date. The Fuscherkarkopf north wall (gradient from 2 in 5 to 1 in 2) had already been descended in 1935. Even in that case one was still talking in terms of a very steep descent. On the other hand, Saudan on his skis had descended the icy flanks of a mountain which the best mountaineers were still trying to conquer, armed with climbing irons and picks, ice-hooks and ice-bolts and with a short fervent prayer that there would be no avalanche.

In 1969 Sylvain Saudan descended the Marinelli on the Monte Rosa east wall. The couloir had not been named after the first people to traverse it (the Englishmen Pendlebury and Taylor, under the leadership of their guide Ferdinand Imseng in 1872), but after Damiano Marinelli, who was torn from his footing by an avalanche during an attempt to climb the same wall in

1881. The air pressure from this avalanche was so strong—or so the story went afterwards—that the body of the guide Imseng, who had accompanied Marinelli too, was found 660 feet above the spot of the accident. In 1970 Sylvain Saudan made a descent over the north-west flank of the Eiger. He arranged to have a helicopter put him down on the summit and his descent was a sensation for the audience watching it on television.

Sylvain Saudan . . . a native of the mountains, who tried to make ski descents where no man had gone before just for his own satisfaction . . . but a man, whom our age was able to transform, within a few years, into a stuntman for the "white sport". For, in the meantime, the sport of skiing had become big business, among those profiting from it being the inhabitants of all those countries where there is a heavy snowfall (an essential factor in maintaining a winter sport); the sport outfitters (a good ski outfit can cost as much as a white collar worker in a high position would earn in a month!); all those who take part in ski races (who can earn plenty of cash from a victory).

Unknown to himself, Sylvain Saudan chose the right time to descend his steep mountainside and, through his action, gave a new stimulus to the sport of skiing. The public always wants the best performance possible. Sylvain Saudan produced it. Just as racing drivers raise the self-confidence of every motorist so, in the same way, the "madman on skis" helps to increase the self-confidence of Mr Everyman trying to descend a gentle meadow-slope on his skiing holiday.

Now Sylvain Saudan is planning to make descents from Aconcagua in the Andes and from Everest.

An invention long since forgotten. The thirring coat, invented over 30 years ago, was supposed to make "hover-skiing" possible.

At over 100 miles per hour on the fastest ski run in the world at Ceruinia.

CHAPTER 10

MOUNTAINS AND MOUNTAINEERING
—PAST AND PRESENT

The mountain that was given away

The twin-peaked Uschba is the wildest and most daunting mountain in the Caucasus. In the language of the natives its name means "mountain of terror". By the year 1888 its north peak (5,360 feet) had been climbed; however, in the following year there were twenty unsuccessful attempts to climb the south peak—only 44 feet higher—by the best climbers of several nations. Finally they said the peak could not be climbed. Was it really unclimbable?

In 1903, three expeditions set off at the same time to conquer the Uschba. Heinrich von Ficker, later a university professor and President of the Academy of Science in Vienna, even took his sister on the expedition, which was led by Willi Rickmer Rickmers. They were almost successful in conquering the mountain.

The roped party was already standing right underneath the snow-field of the summit when Adolf Schulze, who had climbed on ahead, crashed from the rock face in a great curved arc, fell on to the rope and then lay unconscious on a narrow ledge, bleeding profusely from a head wound. The jerk of the rope had burned Heinrich von Ficker's hands right down to the bone when he broke the other man's 60-foot fall and his shoulders had been torn. Rickmer Rickmers and von Ficker's sister Cenzi rescued the two injured men.

They put up a bivouac and returned the next day. Meanwhile another group of German climbers had reached the foot of the mountain. Five days after his terrible fall Schulze—still wearing a bandage on his head—conquered the south peak of the Uschba with this group. Since that time this brave man has been known simply as Schulze of the Uschba, and the courageous Cenzi von Ficker was called the Maid of the Uschba.

The third expedition, consisting of Hans Pfann, Ludwig Distel and Georg Leuchs, all from Munich, arrived a few days too late to make the first ascent. So they made the first crossing of the mountain which meant descending the north peak, then traversing the mountain to the south peak and making their descent from there. The three men were *en route* for a total of five days.

There is something to add: the conquest of the Uschba had a sequel which has never been repeated in the history of climbing. The Prince of Svanetien, Dadechkeliani, was so inspired by the success of the Maid of the Uschba that he made her a present of the mountain. This was not done symbolically, but actually carried

On a snow cornice.

The Uschba. On the left the hotly disputed southern summit and, behind, the northern summit.

was in love with the "heroic" landscape. Of course the travellers were not able to stand the discomforts of an alpine journey in quite the same heroic fashion. After a sleepless night spent on a straw sack full of bugs and fleas, even the most romantic soul became vulnerable. However, the landlords of the primitive country inns soon found that there was a good business to be made out of mountain travellers, and so they provided more comforts. The small country inns expanded into public houses and finally into hotels.

The world's first mountain railway was built between 1848 and 1854 in the Semmering Pass between Lower Austria and Steiermull. While it was being built, the constructor Karl von Ghega was accused of being rash. It was claimed that no one could survive a fast journey at such a height, without suffering damage to his health. Semmering station is situated 2,900 feet above sea level. The rocks hanging over the track would be broken away by the vibrations and they would crush to pieces the trains going past. It was claimed that the trains would stick on the journey up the mountain and that the brakes would fail on the way down. Karl von Ghega was not disconcerted and went on building his railway, although at the time there was still no engine available which could cope with such a steep gradient. Even an international open competition for engine designers was unable to produce a thoroughly satisfactory model. Karl von Ghega was an adventurer, full of energy and confidence in his own luck and then, in the last year of construction, a serviceable locomotive did materialize.

The first mountain railway had scarcely been completed, when the first plans were being drawn up for

through with documents and a seal. Miss Cenzi von Ficker had become the lawful owner of the Uschba.

That was in 1903. Nowadays no one gives mountains away any more, these days they are sold. For instance, since 1957 the Nepalese government has brought in a tariff for mountain climbing. The higher the mountain the higher the price. Meanwhile there have been price rises in the tariffs themselves.

The mountain that was bought

The beginning of the 19th century saw the discovery of the Alps as a place to which to travel. New spiritual undercurrents were evoking a change in people's feelings towards landscapes. Cultivated land was no longer considered beautiful; rather the untouched wilderness was appreciated. The romantic soul

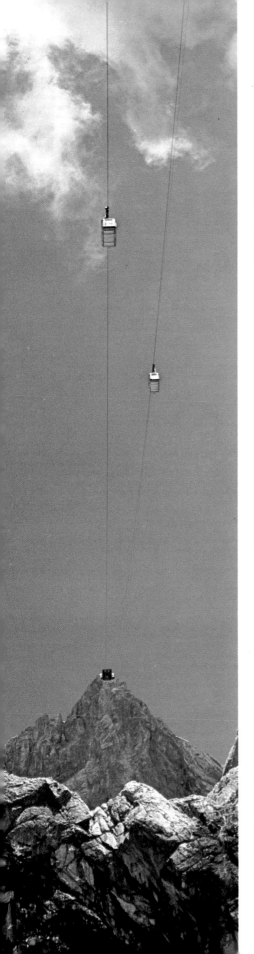

railways to reach mountain peaks. In 1866 the American Sylvester Marsh actually began to build a rack railway on Mount Washington, which is 6,230 feet high, and by 1869 the first railway to reach a mountain summit was completed. Two years later they began to construct a railway using the same system on the Rigi, the mountain which has the most famous vantage point for

The Dachstein cable railway.

Top: *Construction of a viaduct for the Semmering railway (a lithograph of 1850).*

One of the most spectacular roads in the Alps, in the Val d'Annivier, Switzerland.

123

Tents and Buddhist chapels. An expedition strikes camp during an approach march in the Himalayas.

something to which those involved in conveying passengers up the mountains no longer pay any attention. The modern cable-cars fly swift as an arrow, taking their passengers from the low-lying valley stations up to heights of almost 13,000 feet; air-taxis take those who pay them where they want and as high as they want to go.

Poor highlands! that was what people used to say. Nowadays it is mostly the opposite which is correct. Now they are planning to erect a large hotel right at the foot of Mount Everest—the guests will be ferried there and back by air-taxi. In a few decades the Himalayas will probably have been opened up as much as the Alps are today.

The healing mountain

"Mountains make you healthy", was the advice given by Hippolyt Guarinoni to those sick people who came to him for help. Guarinoni was a doctor, scholar, writer and architect who lived in Trienti at the beginning of the 17th century. Mountain climbing as a cure? The people of that time did not understand. It is only now that people are beginning to grasp the fact that the highlands constitute one of the last reserves of good air and tranquillity, that mountain climbing keeps you fit and that you can recover your health, both in body and mind, in the mountains. Of course, many people also die on mountains. Overestimating your own powers and underestimating the mountain is the most common cause of accidents.

However, mountaineering is no more dangerous than driving a car; the subjective as well as objective dangers are the same in both cases. Those who don't take part in any sports at all, and hardly stir, live a life which is essentially more dangerous than that of a mountaineer.

viewing the scenery in Switzerland.

The first ideas for the Rigi railway were pure fantasy. Small wagons on rails would be pulled to the top using balloons! The strangest ideas were explored by people in their efforts to give non-climbers the chance of enjoying the view from the peaks. Someone even wanted to put a pipe through the centre of the mountain and use compressed air to shoot a capsule containing fifty people up to the summit of the Jungfrau, 13,513 feet high—just like a letter sent through the pneumatic post machine. By 1906 they wanted to construct a type of lift through the centre of the Matterhorn, up to its summit. A pressurized observation room placed on the summit was to have protected the passengers from mountain sickness.

Mountain sickness . . . that is

Of course, life does not depend on clambering up vertical rock faces or climbing a 26,000-foot peak. But there have always been people who consider hazards and adventures to be an essential part of their lives. The lust for adventure is not a burden; it is a natural drive, hidden in many people, which demands fulfilment. Mountains have already satisfied the lust for adventure of generations.

"Truly to experience a mountain, you have to spend a night on it", Julius Kugy.

A lonely tent in the icy wastes of the Hindu Kush.

ACKNOWLEDGMENTS

Cover photograph: Guglia Edmondo de Amicis. Foto Ghedina, Cortina d'Ampezzo. Front endpaper: Bearers at the foot of the Nuptse. Back endpaper: Climbers on Kilimanjaro. Both photographs: Bavaria, Munich. Alinari, Florence: p. 20. Ernst Baumann, Bad Reichenhall: p. 41 (top). Jan Boon, Kitzbühel: pp. 59 (top), 61 (top). British Council: p. 54 (bottom). Verlag Bruckmann, Munich: pp. 24 (top), 64, 86 (top). Ed Cooper, Mendocino: p. 91. Kurt Diemberger, Salzburg: pp. 13 (left), 34, 65, 66 (top), 109. Milan Doubek, Hronov: pp. 43, 88. Mario Fantin, Bologna: pp. 49, 52 (top), 53, 100 (top), 101 (top). Wenzel Fischer, Garmisch: p. 78. French Information Service: pp. 62, 63. Hannes Gasser, Innsbruck: pp. 44, 45. L. Gensetter, Davos: p. 73 (centre). Ghedina, Cortina d'Ampezzo: pp. 72, 81, 82 (top). Norbert Hausegger, Graz: p. 73 (top). Toni Hiebeler, Munich: pp. 2, 11 (top and centre), 37, 51, 55, 56, 58 (centre and bottom), 59 (bottom), 70, 82 (bottom), 86 (centre), 89 (right), 90, 112, 120, 124. Rudi Lindner, Pernegg: pp. 13 (both top right), 76 (all five), 77 (bottom), 85, 101 (bottom), 125 (both). Fritzi Lukan, Vienna: pp. 9 (centre and bottom), 16 (top and both bottom), 23 (bottom), 25 (all three bottom), 28 (both), 29, 33 (centre), 74 (top and bottom left), 89 (left), 103 (bottom), 118 (bottom). Reinhold Messner, Villnöss: p. 103. Adi Mokrejs, Vienna: p. 74 (bottom). Fritz Moravec, Vienna: pp. 13 (bottom), 18 (both), 19, 35 (all three), 60 (left), 68 (centre and bottom), 79 (right), 96 (top and bottom), 97, 100 (bottom), 106 (both), 107, 113, 116 (top), 117 (top), 126. Swiss National Tourist Office, Zurich: pp. 32, 40, 41 (top right), 42, 114, 123 (centre). Austrian National Library, Vienna: pp. 12 (top), 24 (bottom), 48, 123 (top). Österreichischer Bundesverlag, Vienna: pp. 8, 12 (bottom), 30, 33 (bottom), 41 (bottom), 50, 52 (bottom), 54 (top left), 73 (bottom), 83 (bottom), 94 (bottom), 108, 116 (bottom), 117 (bottom), 188 (top), 119 (top). Austrian Museum of Applied Art, Vienna: p. 17. Herbert Raditschnig, Salzburg: p. 83 (top). Dölf Reist, Interlaken: pp. 92, 94 (top), 95 (both). Roebild, Frankfurt/Main: p. 14. Kurt Roschl, Vienna: pp. 9 (top), 23 (top), 35 (top left), 36 (top), 54 (top), 61, 67 (top), 75, 77 (top), 79 (left), 80, 87, 104. Schackgalerie, Munich: p. 6. Walter Schaumann, Vienna: p. 25 (top). Karlheinz Schuster, Frankfurt/Main: pp. 98 (top), 99. Alois Sedlacek, Vienna: p. 123 (left). Rudolf Seifert, Dresden: p. 84. Hans Steinbichler, Öd/Hittenkirchen: pp. 10, 11 (bottom), 36 (bottom). Pierre Tairraz, Chamonix: pp. 26, 31, 102. Herbert Tichy, Vienna: p. 68. Hans Truöl, Sonthofen: p. 119 (bottom). Erich Vanis, Vienna: pp. 58 (top), 60 (right), 66 (bottom), 69, 96 (centre), 98 (bottom), 110 (both), 111, 122. Gerhard Watzl, Buenos Aires: p. 105. Zentrale Farbbild-Agentur, Düsseldorf: pp. 38, 46.

FURTHER READING

Blackshaw, A. 1968. *Mountaineering.* Penguin (U.K. and U.S.).
Bonington, C. 1971. *Annapurna South Face.* Cassell (U.K.).
Casewit. C. W. and Pownall. R. 1968. *Mountaineering Handbook: An Invitation to Climbing.* Lippincott (U.S.).
Clark, R. *Great Moments in Mountaineering.* Roy (U.S.).
Crew, P. 1968. *Encyclopaedic Dictionary of Mountaineering.* Constable (U.K.).
Diemberger, K. 1971. *Summits and Secrets.* Allen & Unwin (U.K.).

Engel, C. E. 1971. *Mountaineering in the Alps: an historical survey.* Allen & Unwin (U.K.).
Harrer, H. 1969. *The White Spider.* Hart-Davis (U.K.).
Hornbien, T. F. 1967. *Everest: the West Ridge.* Allen & Unwin (U.K.).
Huxley, A. (Ed.) 1969. *Standard Encyclopedia of the World's Mountains.* Putnam (U.S.).
Morin, N. 1968. *A Woman's Reach.* Eyre & Spottiswoode (U.K.).
Noyce, W. and McMorrin, I. (Eds.) 1970. *World Atlas of Mountaineering.* Macmillan (U.K. and U.S.).
Rébuffat, G. 1967. *On Ice and Snow and Rock.* Kaye & Ward (U.K.).
Shipton, E. G. and Washburn, B. 1966. *Mountain Conquest.* Horizon Caravel Books (U.S.).
Styles, S. (Ed.) 1968. *Men and Mountaineering.* White (U.S.).
Ullman, J. R. 1964. *Age of Mountaineering.* Lippincott (U.S.).
White. A. T. 1962. *All about Mountains and Mountaineering.* Random House (U.S.).

INDEX